SPEND EVERYTHING

Spend Everything

Lonnie R. Mathews

Alliance Financial Ministries

Spend Everything
Copyright © 2002, 2010 Alliance Financial Ministries

www.FinancialMinistries.org

The author has taken reasonable precautions in the preparation of this manual and believes that the facts presented are accurate as of the date written. This publication is designed to provide competent and reliable information regarding the subject matter covered. However, it is sold with the understanding that the author and publisher are not engaged in rendering legal, financial or other professional advice. Laws and practices often vary from state to state and if legal or other expert assistance is required, the services of a professional should be sought. The author and publisher specifically disclaim any liability that is incurred from the use of or application of the contents of this book.

ISBN: 978-0-9826132-1-4 (Softcover)
        978-0-9826132-0-7 (Hardcover)

Cover designed by: EJDesign Firm
Book designed by: Compass Rose Horizons

Acknowledgments

As this book is being formed in my head I want to take this opportunity to acknowledge a few people. First and foremost I would like to give honor to my heavenly Father, without whom none of this would be possible. Next I would like to give mention to the four special ladies in my life. First I would like to acknowledge my soul mate, my better half, the woman who completes me — my wife, Carrie. Your love and support has made life with you the best. Next I would like to acknowledge my dearest mother. Your guidance has kept my path straight and shaped me into the man I am today "Thanks, Mom." Next I would like to acknowledge my reason for waking up every day and living this thing we call life: my two daughters. Corrie, my "ladybug" and Cassie, "Queen Tah-Tah," both of you are part of me forever. While I am sure there are a lot of others who should be acknowledged, the list would be too long to mention. I just want to say thanks to everyone. Thanks to my family and friends whom I interact with on a regular basis.

— *Lonnie Mathews*

Introduction

First let me say thank you for purchasing this book. The fact that you are reading this book tells me a little about you. You are either where you want to be financially and just wanted to read this book for entertainment purposes or you are currently having some challenges financially and are looking for some answers. Let me tell you a little about me and why I wrote this book. This is actually my second book on personal finance, and if I must say so—the best so far.

After almost going broke several years ago I made a decision to go on a never-ending journey to spread the word to individuals regarding personal financial responsibility. When my wife and I graduated from college our combined annual income was over $100K per year. Oddly enough, that was the worst thing that could have ever happened to us; nothing is worse than a lot of money in the hands of the ignorant. It's not that my wife and I were ignorant; after all, we have four academic degrees between us. However, with all of our book knowledge and degrees, we knew nothing about personal finance.

Through my studies I have learned that personal finance is 80 percent personal, and the rest is head knowledge. Because of the passion I have for personal finance I started Alliance Financial Ministries, Inc. (AFM). Through this ministry I teach individuals about personal finance. Alliance Financial Ministries, Inc. is a non-profit organization with a mission to promote financial literacy. It provides financial education programs for individuals and organizations wanting to enjoy a more financially secure future.

As you read the pages of this book, please keep an open mind about the way you view money. You see, most people have views and opinions about money that are based on their life experiences. I was no different; because I grew up in an environment that said "if you want it— get it," no matter what you had to do to get it just get it. That translated in to me making a lot of financial mistakes throughout my life. As I look back, I now realize that those mistakes have probably cost me several hundred thousand dollars.

However, I cannot and will not dwell on the past. There is a saying: "Yesterday is the past, tomorrow is the future, and the greatest present of all is *today*. I truly believe that today is the greatest present of them all. Today is day that you make the decision to change your life forever.

When you are reading this book you will notice that the book is broken up into two distinct parts. Part one is called the "mind set." This part of the book is designed to get you to change your paradigm about money. In other words, the first few chapters are designed to challenge the way you view money. Changing your paradigm is going to require two things. First you are going to have to change who you are; you can't expect to change your situation and still be the same person. I have said to many of my students that with every experience that we go through, we should come out of the experience "different and better." In other words, we shouldn't go through something in life, be it good or bad, and come out of that situation the same person. You shouldn't read this entire book and view your finances the same. The second way to change your paradigm is to do something different; if you aren't where you want to be financially, do something different.

The second part of this book will address key areas of personal finance in which everyone needs to develop healthy habits. This section offers practical advice and information on how to effectively manage your largest wealth building tool—your current income. Over a working lifetime most people will earn over one million dollars. The problem is that most people won't have a whole lot to show for all of the money that will come into their hands.

I hope that these words speak into your life, as I have carefully chosen each word with purpose. Remember to keep an open mind and be receptive to change, because "the only thing that is constant in life is change." – *François de la Rochefoucauld*

Table of Contents

PART ONE: THE MINDSET

"Chaos often breeds life,
when order breeds habit."

— Henry B. Adams

Chaos

It's Friday and it's payday. A few people at the office have decided to go out to lunch. Someone asks if you would like to attend and you say, "Sure. Why not?" On the way to lunch you stop by the ATM machine or maybe you just use your debit card. When you sit down at the table, you figure, "I've got money." After all, you just got paid.

Later that night you get home. It's been a long week. You are tired and don't feel like cooking, so you and your family go out to eat. After all, you just got paid and there is money in your account. You wake up on Saturday and you have a lot of running around to do, so you pack up the kids and begin your day. By now it's past noon and you and the kids are starving so what do you do? You grab a quick bite to eat. Also, while you are out you see a couple things on sale, and you just can't resist. After all, it's on sale and you just got paid. Because you were busy running errands all day, you are not even going to think about cooking, so you order pizza, hot wings, and cokes. Later, on Sunday evening after waking up from your nap, you start getting ready for your week. You know the usual, getting the kid's clothes ironed, getting your stuff together, and oooh, you say to for yourself, "I need to pay my bills." You sit down, gather your bills, and add them all up—at least the minimum payments.

You are not going to even think about paying more than that right now. You log on to check your account balance online and see that most of the purchases that you made over the last couple days have cleared your account except for one or two. You subtract the ones that haven't cleared your account and any other pre-authorized debits from your account to see how much you have left to use for paying your other bills. Most people have the big items taken automatically from their account—things like the house note and car payment. It's the smaller bills that we tend not to notice.

As you sit there it is at that moment when you realize that you should have paid more attention to your account and what you were spending over the weekend. Oh well, there is nothing that you can do about now. You just have to pay what you can. So you start the *"Robbing Peter to pay Paul"* process. Your light bill is $122.44, so you pay only a small amount, such as $72.00. You continue this process with all of the other bills, because if you paid everyone you wouldn't have any money left-over. Let's not forget that you will need gas next week, money for those days when you don't feel like fixing your lunch (which is most days), and money for your morning coffee. You will also need to give the kids money for this, that, and the other. So, some of your bills won't get paid. You say to yourself that next payday you will get things caught up. The thing about next payday is that it's always next payday, so you continue this process, just hoping that nothing comes up in the meantime.

You continue the bill shuffle during the months when the weather is nice and your power bill is not that high. The carry-over balance continues to grow each month because you never can seem to get the bills caught up. Now, the next few months you are still managing to get by. Things are not the best, but hey, at least you are making it. When the power bill comes you noticed that it is *pink*, which usually means that it is past due. The power company has been patient up until this point, but now they want all of their money or your service will be disconnected. So, on Sunday as you do your usual bill shuffle, you decide to not pay the gas bill and cheat a little on your cell phone bill to get the power bill caught up before they cut you off. Keep in mind that you have also been cheating these bills as well, so you are only making a bad situation worse. A few days later, just before payday, you go to make a call on your cell phone and get sent directly to the Verizon operator.

Dang. I was going to pay the bill in a couple of days when I got paid.

They inform you that your service has been interrupted

for non-payment. You are a little angry, but there is nothing you can do, and you really *need* your phone (not really). So you continue to make things worse by giving the operator your debit card number, so that you can get your service back. As you are giving the number to the agent, in the back of your mind, you realize deep down that there is not enough money in your account to cover this. The only thing that you can hope for at this point is that one of those checks for some other bill doesn't come through before your direct deposit hits in a couple days.

Sure enough, on the day before payday, you decide to check your account online to make sure everything is okay. While entering the password you are quietly praying that you haven't bounced anything, but no such luck. Indeed, the check that you wrote to your child's daycare bounced, and you were already a day late paying the bill anyway. So now you have a negative balance in your account and a bad check at your child's daycare that you will have to take care of, plus a returned check fee. You sit there staring at the computer screen, looking at your checking account balance, and think to yourself that you are glad tomorrow is payday.

One of these days I am going to get my act together ...

If you are like most people, this story hits very close to home. This is the story of millions of Americans who find themselves caught in this perpetual cycle of just getting by, payday after payday. Studies show that more than 70 percent of all Americans are living from paycheck to paycheck. You see, over time we just get use to living what I like to call controlled chaos. This situation is chaotic at best, but most people live their lives like this. As you were reading this story, you were probably thinking: *This is me. How did he know that this is what I go through week after week?* The reason that I know this story all too well is because that was my life before my eyes were opened. My eyes were opened to a new way of living, a new way of looking at my money. This new way of thinking required me to make the decision that I wasn't going to continue to live my life the way I was living it. I was always uneasy about my financial situation, but for a long time, I was not uncomfortable enough to do anything about it. Finally, I developed a five-part strategy that changed my financial future—and it can change yours too.

Now, before I reveal this plan to you, I have to warn you that there are no big secrets involved. In fact, after you read the plan you might think to yourself, that's nothing new. I knew that already. My question then is if you knew this already, then why haven't you done anything about your situation?

Okay. Here we go; here is the five part strategy to change your financial future:

1. Think net worth.
2. Set financial goals.
3. Spend less than you earn.
4. Save regularly.
5. Reduce and eliminate debt.

That's it; if you start to implement this five-part plan into your everyday financial life, you will see a change in your current situation. I have been living this plan for the past eight years, and I can honestly say that my life hasn't been the same since.

At first glance these concepts may seem simple at best, but sometimes simple is the best option. Often, after doing a seminar or workshop, I would have someone come up to me and ask, "Does this stuff really work?" My answer is always, "Yes." There are no shortcuts and no secrets. Now let me shed some light on these basic principles to make sure you really understand them.

Think net worth. When it comes to net worth, most people don't think about it much. The basic concept to thinking net worth is that whenever you are considering a major purchase (and sometimes a not-so-major purchase), you should ask yourself: *How is this going to affect my net worth?* To determine how this is going to affect your net worth, you must first understand what your net worth is. The formula to calculate your net worth is ASSETS – LIABILATIES = NET WORTH. This is the basic accounting formula for determining your net worth.

- Assets = The things that you own
- Liabilities = The people you owe

From now on, when considering making a large purchase, ask yourself: *Is this going to increase or decrease my net worth if I purchase this item?* If the answer is that it will decrease your net worth, is it really worth it?

Set financial goals. Setting financial goals is a very important step in truly achieving financial freedom. Every successful person who has ever accomplished anything set some goals along the way. To get to where you want to be financially, you have to first know where you want to go. This concept is so important that there is a section dedicated to helping you set and achieve financial goals.

Spend less than you earn. At first glance this concept may seem simple, but it has proven to be very difficult to accomplish. The concept of spending less than you earn requires you to re-introduce a word back in to your vocabulary that most people have forgotten. That word is no! To regularly spend less than you earn, you must learn to say no more often. Let's practice. On the count of three, I want you to yell very loudly and enthusiastically: No!

1-2-3 … No! I will not continue to spend more than I make, No! I won't continue to jeopardize my future by spending money that I don't currently have, No! I don't want to continue to live my life the way I am. I think you get the point.

Save regularly. I once read a book called The richest man in Babylon by George S. Clauson, and it was the story of the richest man in Babylon. Someone once asked how he became the richest man in Babylon, and his response was, "I learned early on that a tenth of all that I earn is mine to keep." Just the very thought of saving money has escaped our society. The latest statics state that Americans have a negative saving rate. What? How can you have a negative saving rate? It's easy when you consider that most Americans spend $1.22 for every dollar that they earn. To change your life, you have to save money regularly.

Reduce and eliminate debt. To truly escape the past, you have to rid yourself of all the payments from past decisions and start down a new path. Start down a path that doesn't include you financing things that you really don't need. Let's face it, how would your life be different if you didn't have all the payments that you currently have? Imagine getting your paycheck and the only bills you had were your everyday living expenses. What if you didn't have the car payment that you now have? What if you didn't have to make the minimum payment on those credit cards? What if you didn't have that student loan payment that you are making after having graduated from college ten years ago? To ever get where you want to be financially, you have to develop a plan to reduce and eliminate all debt from your current financial life.

*"Being rich is having money;
being wealthy is having time"*

— Margaret Bonnano

Wealth is a Journey

Let's talk for a few moments about wealth or being wealthy. First let me say that I believe that wealth is a journey rather than a point in time. It's a process; it's a state of mind that takes continued effort to obtain and maintain, but most of all, wealth is relative.

Yes. It is relative—not your relative being wealthy and you not being wealthy (sorry I couldn't resist). What I mean is that you don't necessarily have to be a multimillionaire to be considered wealthy. Being wealthy is not based on how much you have, but rather what you do with what you have. I am convinced that people with lots of money are not or can't be any happier than those who don't have lots of money.

I refuse to believe that having *money* is the basis of my happiness. Don't get me wrong. I do realize that having money will make life more enjoyable, but not happier. All of that is to say that wealth is relative to your lifestyle needs.

If you lead a modest lifestyle, a life where you are person-ally happy with where you are in life, and you some how manage to live below your means financially, then two things will happen.

(1) You will live a much happier life.
(2) You will build wealth over time.

Making a lot of money doesn't make people wealthy, especially if their expenses are equal to their income, or in some cases exceed their income. A person may look wealthy and smell wealthy, but it doesn't mean they are wealthy. How many times have you seen someone in a fancy car—let's say a foreign luxury car—and thought: *That person must have a lot of money.* Did you realize that the foreign luxury cars that are leased outnumber the foreign luxury cars that are sold? So is this person really wealthy? Anyone with a calculator and common sense can figure out that leasing is the worst way to own, or should I say *drive* an automobile.

If you are not currently wealthy and you would like to become wealthy, then you only have to do one thing, and that thing is change! If you are not where you want to be financially, physically, emotionally, or spiritually, all you have to do is *change*. Change everything about you—the people you meet, the books you read, and most of all, the habits that are currently a part of your everyday routine. If you want to change your financial life, you must change the way you are doing things, and the reason you must change is because *what you are doing is not working!*

If there is to be any difference in your financial life, you cannot be the same person doing the same thing and expecting something different. The first thing you should change is your paradigm of thinking. What I mean is, you should think of your personal finances as if you are running a small business. The businesses income is your salary and the business expenses are your current monthly bills, and they need to be managed.

Imagine for a moment that you were a CEO of a company, and someone in the finance department was handling the business finances the way you are currently handling them. Would you fire that person? Maybe you would; maybe you wouldn't. But if the company is not going in the direction that it should, you would agree that something needs to be changed. If your company has gotten off track financially, you must fire your old self and hire a new you.

Every business that is successful has a net profit each month, which is money left over at the end of each month to invest back into the business. You must examine your financial situation and see whether you have a net profit or loss every month. Think of yourself as the CEO and the CFO, and you must get this company on the right track financially. Many of the world's wealthiest individuals think of both their personal finances and their business finances in terms of income, expenses and profits.

Do you have what it takes to be rich?

Being rich or having wealth is a state of mind. In addition to it being a state of mind, it's a thought process and a series of habits that keep you pointed in the right direction. The path to wealth is a relative easy one. All you have to do is spend less than you earn and save regularly—and that's it. Over time you will build wealth, so why there aren't more wealthy people than there are in the world? The truth is that most people lack the willingness to change their current lifestyles and spending habits. Remember, building wealth is a way of life; it's like getting into really good physical shape. To stay in shape, you have to continue to do the things that got you into shape in the first place.

Most people also lack the discipline to become wealthy. It's not easy to change what you have been doing most of your life. You have to develop a level of "stick-to-it-ness." Most people just give up too easily. There are also a lot of misconceptions when it comes to building wealth, such as, *if I were wealthy, my problems would go away. More people would like me if I had money,* and *if I were wealthy, I could buy anything that I wanted.* Part of what makes wealthy people wealthy is their ability to say, "No."

The difference between being wealthy and middle-class is being able to afford anything you want, but choosing not to anyway. When I was broke, I would go the mall and buy anything that I wanted, even if it meant that I had to buy it on credit, or I would say things such as, "When I get some money I'm going to buy …." In other words, I really couldn't afford it in the first place, but I bought it anyway. Now that I have a higher level of understanding about money and I have developed discipline and good habits, I could go to the same mall and have the ability to purchase just about anything in there that I wanted, but I choose not to, instead. That's what makes me wealthy; because of my new attitude, I am wealthier in a lot of ways.

Attitude of abundance

We can change our lives by changing our attitudes. With a new attitude comes a new outlook; a new outlook will change your actions. If you believe that you can't or won't ever have wealth, then you're right you won't. Building wealth is about believing that you can build wealth, and then going out and doing the things that will build wealth. You must have an attitude of abundance, and then you will have abundance.

What keeps many of us from doing something new is the fear of failure. Imagine the possibilities you would have in life if you didn't fear failing. One day my wife made the comment, "On any given day, most people don't give life their best, because they might fail." I think what she was trying to say is that we don't try hard, because we wonder what will happen if we try our best and still fail? How would you react if you tried your best and your best wasn't good enough? So, for that reason, most of us don't try hard; that way we can always say, "Well, I didn't try very hard, anyway." I think that most of us don't try hard, because we might actually succeed. What would happen if we really tried hard to do something and succeeded? Then what? You can't just go back to what you were doing; you will have to look for another challenge.

Try This…

Make a short list of three things that you would absolutely do if you knew you would accomplish them without failing. Go ahead. Write down three things that you would do if you knew that there was no way possible for you to fail. Now, write a plan to achieve those three things. Now, ask yourself what's holding you back.

All too often we get stuck in our comfort zone, and that's what keeps us trapped in our current position. It's those comfort zones that keep us from achieving our goals. I like to say: *Until the pain of your current situation becomes greater than the pain of change, you won't change.* I want to challenge you to get out of your comfort zone. Do something different. Do something that you always wanted to do. Go ahead. I dare you to try. Don't be afraid to make a mistake. Don't be afraid of failure. *To succeed is to fail and to fail is to succeed.* Making mistakes is the opportunity to learn. Mistakes teach you what not to do the next time you try—that is if you try a next time. One of the biggest reasons people aren't wealthy is because they never tried. If you find yourself off course because of a mistake, just retrace your steps, find the mistake, make the necessary corrections, and keep moving forward. Remember, wealth is a journey, not a destination. You must make the decision to seek wealth, and if you do, then you will find it. You do have to take the first step on a life journey, though.

"Comfort zones are the distance between your fear of failure and your fear of SUCCESS!"

— Lonnie R. Mathews

Get Off the Nail!

One day there was a salesmen traveling in a rural area, and he came upon a farm. The salesman drove down the long gravel driveway. Once he got to the house, he noticed an older gentleman sitting on the porch in a rocking chair. To the man's side was an even older hound dog. The salesman got out of his car and approached the old man to tell him about the products that he was selling. Once the salesman got to the porch, he was greeted, and he sat next to the old man and the hound dog. Here is where the story gets interesting. The salesman noticed that every now and then the hound dog would move and then let out a small whimper. This happened several times during the conversation, and the old man never did anything. So the salesman finally asked the old man, "Why is it that every time that your dog moves, he whimpers?" The old man replied, "He's lying on a nail." So the salesman continued to have a conversation with the old man, and after a couple more times of the dog moving and whimpering, the salesman asked the old man, "Sir, let me ask you why your dog doesn't just get off of the nail?" The old man replied, "I guess it don't hurt him enough." I like to use this illustration often, especially when I am doing a seminar or workshop on personal finance. You see, most people are in love with the idea of being financially free. Not necessarily rich, but financially free to do the things that you really want to do. But I have found that most people aren't willing to do the things that are necessary to get there.

So the nail in the story is a metaphor for anything that keeps you from doing what it is that you really want to do. The nail could represent anything; it could be that you have bad financial habits, spiritual issues; relationship issues—any number of things. The thing about the nail is that you know it is there, and it hurts you, yet you haven't made the decision to do anything about it. Many of us are like the dog; we just want to lay there and whimper and hope that someday something will change, through no effort of our own, of course.

You won't change until the pain of your current situation becomes greater than the pain of change.

And your situation could be anything that you are having difficulty with, yet refuse to do anything about it. Let's face it. If your life isn't where you want it to be, who can you blame? The truth is *you*. I know that may sound a little self-righteous, but it is true. If things aren't going your way, then change. Every day that you wake up, you have the power to change. You can change your mind, your habits, and ultimately your life. Virtually everyone once possessed an unshakable spirit that his or her life was going to be special and unique.

Do you remember when you were in high school and you thought that you were invincible? You had conviction that you would somehow go out and capture a lifetime full of dreams that would one day become a reality. But something has happened along the way. Through it all, the process of life seemed to get in the way. Maybe it was one bad decision after another that has kept you from achieving those dreams that you were once so passionate about.

Now, here you are. You have somehow realized that those dreams, like so many other things in life are very fragile and so easily lost. Then we end up settling for a fraction of the life that we thought we wanted—a fraction of what could have been and what we could have. You wake one day and realize that your life is full of nothing more that a bunch of broken dreams and promises.

So what do you do?

While there are a lot of things that you could do when you are in such a situation, and the answer would be different depending on the area of your problems. I am convinced that a lot of the problems that most people have can be traced back to their finances. The reason that we don't get off the nail is because we have lost hope that things will get better, or maybe we just don't want to change. Sometimes the fear of the unknown is greater than the pain we currently feel.

So my solution on what to do when you find yourself surrounded by a bunch of broken dreams and promises is simple: *change!* It is now time to design the next ten years of your life. If you are like most people, a significant part of the money that you currently earn is going to satisfy some past debt or obligation. In other words:

Your past decisions are haunting your present, and if you aren't careful, they can jeopardize whatever future that you might have.

You must first put aside all vestiges of personal debt. If you are one of those individuals who somehow think that next year is going to be different, then you are engaging in self-delusion. For your future to be any different than your past or your present, you have to become a different person.

You have to go on the offense against the burdens of personal debt. It is debt that stands in the doorway of your future. It is debt that keeps you from achieving those dreams that you were once passionate about. It is debt that stands guard on the path of your fortune. You must do everything in your power to cast it aside. To start this march on the road to financial freedom, you have everything you need. You don't need more experience, you don't need more knowledge. All you need is to recapture the unshakable spirit that you once had. In life, sometimes we as humans tend to continue to do things that we should have left undone and leave undone the things we should have done.

To escape the trap of debt, you have to take a new interest in INTEREST. Either you are paying interest to someone else or you are earning it for yourself.

To become different, you have to decide that today is the day; it's the day that I change my life for ever. From this moment on, commit yourself to two things:

1. You will cast aside the anchors of the past, including all the debt associated with the past.
2. Next, you must embark upon a new journey leading to a new and better destination.

The biggest reason for failure is that we tend to spend all that we earn, but a few dollars saved each month and invested can make a person wealthy in his or her lifetime. With every dollar that you earn, you must learn to pay yourself first. No one is more important than you; if a person keeps one tenth of all he earns for himself in ten periods, he would have the equivalent of one whole.

Let me break that down a little. If I earn four hundred dollars each week, and I keep for myself 10 percent, or forty dollars, then in ten weeks I would have one week's worth of income saved. How would having one week's, one month's or even one year's income saved change your life? But when we have debt in our lives, we can't comply with this very basic principle, and if we can't comply now, well when we will be able to comply. The answer is that if you don't make the commitment, then you will never comply. *Every repeated human act becomes a habit.*

Every day your thoughts should be on how you can change your situation for the better, because:

> *Your thoughts become your words;*
> *Your words become your actions,*
> *Your actions become your habits,*
> *Your habits becomes your character,*
> *and your character determines your success.*

—Frank Outlaw

"Success is the reward for persistence!"

— David Cottrell

Persistence:
Going Beyond the Splat!

There was once a man on a road to success, and he came to a fork in the road. One road will take him to sure success, and the other will take him to failure. So the man needed to make a choice. However, the man noticed that standing at the fork in the road was a guru (a person who knows all).

So the man asked the guru, "Kind sir, could you point me in the direction of success." Standing there for what seemed an eternity, the guru finally pointed in a particular direction. The man, thrilled at the possibility of being successful beyond his wildest dreams, went in that direction

All of a sudden, a few moments later, there was a loud "SPLAT" sound. Eventually the man came limping back, tattered and stunned. The man went to the guru and said, "Sir, I must have made a mistake somewhere. I was wondering if you could once again point me in the direction of success." Standing there with his frail body, the guru still didn't speak, but he pointed in the same direction. Now, certain that he had it right this time, the man went off in that direction excited about the possibility of being successful beyond his wildest dreams. A few moments later, just as before, there was an even louder "SPLAT" sound. This time the man crawled back to the fork in the road, and not only was he stunned and tattered, but his body was broken and bleeding.

With frustration in his voice, the man screamed to the guru, "Look, I asked you to point me in the direction of success. Well, I followed your instructions, and all I have gotten is splatted! No more pointing. Please just speak to me and tell me which way to success."

After standing there for a while the guru finally spoke and said: "Success is in the direction that I sent you, the only problem is that it's on the other side of the SPLAT."

How many times have you set out to do something with the hopes of being successful, only to find that you might have misjudged the task? In life there is really no such thing as an instant success. It may appear that a person is an overnight success, because you might have just heard of them. What you didn't see is all of the hard work that was put in to get to that point.

Success is the reward for persistence.

Often times after doing a seminar or workshop on budgeting, I would have an individual come up to me and say, "I tried to budget my money, but it's just too hard." I would say that person did not give it enough time. Normally it will take about ninety days for a budget to work. Let's face it. You didn't develop bad money habits over night, so what makes you think that you will change those habits overnight?

Being persistent is about sticking to something and learning from your failures. It's about making the choice to be persistent; even in the face of failure. Unlike the man in the story, becoming successful is having the guts to continue forward, even when you have been splattered.

Persistence is about making the choice to set some goals and reaching those goals; it's about coming to a roadblock and figuring a way over or around or sometimes through an obstacle. By definition, *an obstacle IS something, material or nonmaterial, that stands in the way of literal or figurative progress*. Notice that an obstacle doesn't prevent success; it only impedes or gets in the way of success. In the end, you have the power within you to become a success; you just have to make the choice to figure out a way past the obstacles that are often found along the way. The difference between an obstacle and an excuse is what you choose to do when faced with a challenge. Successful people merely have obstacles on the way to success; those who give up make excuses. By definition, an excuse is justification why something didn't happen.

If you didn't get paid to do your job, would you do it?

I often ask this question during one of my seminars as a test of where you are. You see, most people would respond to that question by saying, "No." I would then ask, "Then why are you there?" People generally have several reasons, one of which is lack of direction or goals. But the most prevalent reason is that most people can't afford to do what they truly wanted to do because of *debt*.

I would encourage you to be persistent in your pursuit to become debt free, so that you can do what you truly love to do. I can honestly say that there is nothing more fulfilling in life than doing what you truly love. Every day that I awake I am thankful that I have the opportunity to do something that I really enjoy doing *(which is speak to people)*, and the amazing thing is, I usually get paid to do it.

It's about discovering what it is that you are passionate about; it's about discovering what you would like to do even if you didn't get paid to do it. What is it for you? What is the thing that you really value doing with your time? That is your passion. Most people don't know what they are passionate about, much less try to do it fulltime. After you address you financial obstacles and you figure out a way around, over, or through your obstacles, then you will be free to discover a new you; free to discover your true, passion in life.

Once you develop a plan to change your life financially, stay committed to the plan. Don't let anyone or anything distract you. You have to be committed to seeing this journey to the end; you have to develop the *burn the ship* mentality. There was a story of a ship captain that was getting ready for battle. The captain and his men boarded their ships and sailed across the seas to do battle with the enemy. Once the men and all of their equipment were safely off the ship, the captain gave the order to burn the ship. As the ship was burning, the captain gathered the men and said, "We are here to fight and win; there will be no retreat. The only way off this island and back home with your loved ones is victory, because we have no ship to retreat to.

> *"Personal progress comes to those who learn to take personal responsibility for the quality of their lives, and who step forth with the determination to make themselves truly unique."*

> — Cyril Parkinson

Parkinson's Law

Have you ever gotten a raise and wondered what happened to it? According to a study by benefits consultants Mercer Human Resource Consulting, employers granted average pay raises of 3.7% in 2006.

So what does that mean to you and me? According to the latest US census, the average salary in the US is $50,233. Therefore, if you were granted a 3% raise, you would receive an extra $1,547 next year, which comes out to approximately $128 dollars per month extra. Granted, by the time you take into account taxes, you really don't get that full amount. My question is what happens to that extra money that you get?

Think back over your working life; think about all of the raises that you have ever gotten. What happen to them? Did they just seem to disappear? Of course they did. I recently had a conversation with a good friend named Arel Moodie, who, by the way, is a successful entrepreneur.

We were discussing finance, and he mentioned a theory called *"Parkinson's Law."* I wasn't sure what the theory was at the time, but I let on like I did. After I got back home, I did some research on the theory, and I must admit I found it very interesting. Parkinson's Law was first articulated by Cyril Parkinson. It turns out that Mr. Parkinson wrote an essay in 1955 that stated that, "Work expands so as to fill the time available for its completion." Though the research mainly dealt with the work levels of civil service workers, the essay was later published as a book that went on to become a bestseller. The theory in the book *Parkinson's Law* can be summarized by saying:

The demand upon a resource always expands to match the supply of the resource.

"What does that have to do with me and my money?" you might be asking. Well, everything. Think about it this way. Your current income is a supply of money that you earn each week, month, and year. Your expenses are the resources that eat away at your supply of money. So from a personal financial perspective, you could state Parkinson's Law by saying:

Your expenses rise to meet your current income.

What could be truer? Otherwise, how else do you account for all the raises that you have gotten over the years, and your life hasn't changed for the better? Maybe it has.

I'm not sure, but for the many people, it hasn't. Look back at your life. Compare your salary now to what you earned ten years ago, or maybe even five years ago, that is, if you have been working that long. I am sure that you will find a significant difference in the amount of money you made compared to what you make now. Sure you have nicer things, and you should have nice things. However, how do you honestly feel about your financial situation at this point? Could you have done things a little differently?

Most people feel that way. I know I do. The truth is that even if you don't make a lot of money, you have the potential to make millions of dollars over your working life time. An individual who earns $25,000 per year and gets a small 3 percent raise each year will earn more than $1.2 million dollars over a thirty-year working life. The biggest question is how much of that $1.2 million will you have when you are done working? Or will you be like everyone else who says, "Man, it sure was fun!"? I personally want better for myself, for my family, and for my legacy.

For financial independence to be achieved, we must first put aside all vestiges of personal debt. Making money is seldom the problem. It is what we do with what we earn, and what we become in the process that will ultimately determine the true value of our life. Owing money to other people obligates us to give our hard-earned money to them, sometimes even before we give to ourselves. To accumulate wealth, we have to become our most important creditor, more important than anyone else we owe.

Conventional wisdom states that the first ten percent of every dollar that we earn should be put aside and paid to ourselves.

However, when debt is present or you have a lot of expenses, you cannot always comply with this rule. If there isn't enough money to pay yourself before you pay your creditors, and after you have taken care of your daily essentials, then it is imperative that you find a way. If your future is going to be different than your past or the present, you must make it so. You have to seize every opportunity you have to lower your expenses. If you cannot comply with this simple act, then you will never achieve financial independence. Every repeated human act becomes a new discipline, and those same acts become new habits.

The biggest reason for human failure is that we tend to spend all that we earn; but a hundred dollars each month, set aside and invested, can make a poor person wealthy in her lifetime. You can have more than you have, because you can become more than you are; but success comes before work only in the dictionary. The *pay yourself first* process requires you to have the unshakable discipline to pay yourself each and every month, without exception and without fail. However, for most people, paying themselves seems like an impossible dream.

Choices

With every dollar that comes into our lives we have a choice. We have the choice on how the dollars that we have earned today will shape our lives tomorrow. What we do with the dollars that we earn will determine whether we will be rich, poor, or middle class in the future. In the book, *The Millionaire Next Door,* authors Dr. Thomas Stanley and Dr. William Danko discovered some amazing facts about individuals who started with little or no wealth and over time accumulated a net worth of more than one million dollars. There were two things that all of these individuals had in common, no matter what their backgrounds were or how they accumulated their wealth.

Number one was that they lived well below their means and were very frugal with their money. The study showed that the average self-made millionaire drove a two- to three-year-old car. The second thing that individuals who became millionaires did to become wealthy was that they spent their time and resources on ways to build wealth. In other words, these individuals didn't waste a lot of their time purchasing and displaying high status items. This means that they didn't purchase status items like expensive luxury cars and over- the-top homes.

The first choice that you must make if you ever want to become wealthy is to control your spending. I realize that may sound easy, but trust me, it is a very difficult thing to accomplish. Controlling and ultimately reducing your current spending means that you must control the desire to consume. Let's face it. No one ever sets out to overspend; they just don't have a plan not to overspend. Controlling the desire to consume is a lot of work, especially when you consider that every minute of the day we are bombarded with advertisements from companies jockeying for your hard-earned dollars. When you think about it, there are really only three things that you can do with the money that you earn. (1) You could spend it. (2) You could save or invest it. (3) You could give it away. No matter what action you take with money, it will fall into one of these three areas. The trick to being financially wealthy is to find a healthy balance among the three.

Most people focus all of their time on the spending part and not enough on the saving and giving parts. If you ever want to get ahead financially, you must learn to control your spending. Unfortunately, just like Parkinson's Law, our everyday expenses tend to rise to meet our income. As soon as you get a raise or some additional income, you find ways for it to become consumed. Make today the day you take a stance against overspending. Today is the day you draw a line in the sand, and today is the day you say, "No more." Once you have the attitude that you want to change, here's what you do. Take a serious look at your current spending and decide on some areas that you could cut. At first glance you my say, "Hey, there is nothing to cut; I need to spend money on the things that I am spending it on now." Really, do you absolutely need all those cable channels? Do you really need that gym membership, because you go to the gym every day, right? I think you get the point. There are thousands of ways to cut your spending, and there are plenty of books and articles out there for you to read and come up with ways to reduce your spending. The trick is that you really have to want to reduce your spending and change your lifestyle to get where you want to be financially. The main reason that you don't have more money saved—the main reason that you aren't where you want to be financially is you!

To conquer life we must first conquer ourselves.

I like this quote because it sums up most people's financial problems in a very short and to-the-point statement. This statement simply says that for your financial life to get where you want it to be, you must find a way to control your spending. That means that you must find a way to control you. I could go on and on about how to control your spending and finding ways to cut back, but I won't. I will leave that up to you to decide when and where you will control your spending and change your life.

More isn't always the answer.

Often times when an individual is having financial problems she somehow convinces herself that she just needs to make more money. As I mentioned earlier in the chapter, according to Parkinson's Law your expenses rise to meet your income.

This happens as in the previous example of getting raise after raise on your job, and still not managing to get ahead financially. When times get tight financially, most people think the best way to improve their cash flow issue is to get a second job. Getting a second or part-time job may or may not help. It really depends on your current circumstances. If you are earning a very low wage and are having a hard time making ends meet, then a second job could definitely help. However, if you already make a decent salary and just haven't figured out a way to control your spending, a second job won't help.

There are several factors involved with getting a second job, especially if you have other goals, objectives and obligations that you are dealing with. When you take into consideration the effect of taxes, it will take more extra income to get the same effect of simply cutting back on your current spending. For example, let's assume that you took a part-time job earning $8 per hour, and you worked an additional twenty hours per week on that job, which is a lot. That would mean that you would earn an additional $160 per week. After federal and social security taxes you would net $140 per week (assuming you were single with zero exemptions and didn't have to pay state taxes). Wouldn't it just be easier to look at your current spending to figure out ways to reduce your spending by $140 each week? If you could give up, say cable or some other luxury item, you would have the same cash flow effect of working twenty hours per week. The best part about reducing your spending is that you wouldn't have to work and additional twenty hours to get an extra $140. Reducing your spending is one of the most effective ways to change your financial picture, but first we must change the one thing that is keeping you where you are financially, and that is *you*.

Part Two: The Journey

"The art of saving has been lost in a society of instant gratification."

— Lonnie R. Mathews

Saving

Another year has come and gone. You are probably doing what millions of Americans all across the United States are doing. You more than likely say to yourself, "I can't believe that I spent as much as I did during the holidays!" Now that you are starting a new year once again, let me ask you something: *How much did you save last year?*

Most of us wish we could save more—or maybe not. Maybe you are one of those individuals who always save a certain percentage of his income every year. According to the Christian Science Monitor, in 2006 the US personal savings rate as a percent of disposable income is less than 1 percent.

The truth is that we as Americans are not saving; studies show that more than 70 percent of working individuals are living from paycheck to paycheck. Most financial planners will tell you that you need to save.

It's not just the act of saving, but it's how you save that is the most important part. There is an art to savings, and it should be done correctly. I want to take few pages to share with you a time-tested technique that will help you save money should you choose to accept the challenge. The number one thing you need to implement a successful savings program is a goal. Often times the reason that we don't save is that we never set a goal to save. Not only should we have a goal, but it should also be: (1) *specific* (2) *measurable* and (3) *achievable*.

You should have a specific amount in mind that you want to have saved by a specific time period. Because this concept is new to most people, let's start slowly. Say you want to save $2,000 by the end of a year. This is certainly a worthwhile goal; imagine if you had $2,000 in a savings account. How much better would your life be? If the car broke down, you would just get it fixed. If an unexpected emergency happened, you would just deal with it, and it wouldn't be a problem. I am convinced that when unexpected things happen, they aren't necessarily emergencies. When the unexpected happens, it's only an emergency when you don't have the money to take care of the situation. If you do, however, have the money to take care of the situation, then it's only an inconvenience.

The difference between an inconvenience and an emergency is a savings account.

Just what would it take to save $2,000 by the end of one year? Start by taking the $2,000 and dividing it by twelve months. That gives you $166.66 per month. (If you like, you could divide it by the number of paydays between now and end of one year.) If you get paid bi-weekly, then you would need to save $76 per payday. Now that you have a goal and a specific plan of action, what is next? How do you get from point A (no savings) to Point B (having $2,000 or whatever amount you choose in a saving account for emergencies)? The one reason that most people don't achieve their savings goal is that they save in the wrong order.

When most people set out to save, they already have several monthly financial obligations that are eating at their monthly cash flow. So by the time they pay everybody that they owe, they have very little left for themselves. That is why most people fail to meet their savings goals; they lack the self-discipline to do what they set out to do. Things just happen. That item that you've had your eye on goes on sale. You don't feel like cooking tonight, or you had a bad week at work, and you self-medicate by shopping. All of those can be reasons why people don't save.

To overcome this potential problem, you must pay yourself first (PYF). In other words you are your most important creditor. Try this. Set up an automatic saving plan; think about your retirement savings plan. Those of you who actually participate in company-sponsored retirement savings, you would be surprised to know how many people don't. (I'll save that conversation for another time). If you do participate, you will remember when you first started. You thought to yourself, "I don't know how I will be able to save and live." But now that you have been doing it for a while, you most likely don't even miss the money coming out of your paycheck. The same concept should be applied to your regular savings plan. The only difference is that you won't have to wait until retirement to access some of your money.

To set up an automatic saving plan (ASP), the process is pretty simple. First, you have several options to choose from. You could use your local bank and receive a small amount of interest on your savings, you could go with an online savings account such as with Capital One online or ING online or you could choose a mutual fund money market account. All of these are good options; I would recommend that you do some research to see which option works best for you. The benefit of setting up an account at an online bank or at a mutual fund company is that you don't have immediate access to your money. I didn't say that you don't have access; you just don't have immediate access. If you use one of these options it will typically take a couple days for the money to show up in your checking account. That gives you time to come up with an alternative way to handle the current emergency.

Do Something Different to Become Different.

Saving money is not a matter of math. You will not save money when you get that next raise. You will not save money when that car is paid off. You will not save money when the kids are grown. You will only save money when it becomes an emotional priority. We all know we need to save, but most people don't save as they know they need to save. Why? Because they have competing goals. The goal to save isn't a high enough priority to delay that purchase of the pizza, a DVD player, a new computer, or a china cabinet. So we purchase, buy, consume all our dollars away or worse yet, go into debt to buy these things. That debt means monthly payments control our paychecks and make us say things such as, "We just don't make enough to save any money!" Wrong, wrong, wrong! We do make enough to save money; we just aren't willing to quit spoiling ourselves with our little projects or pleasures to have enough left to save. I don't care what you make; you can save money. It just has to become a big enough priority to you.

If a doctor told you that you were dying and could only be saved with a $5,000 operation that your insurance would not cover and you had 9 months from today to come up with the money, could you save $5,000? Yes! Of course you could! You would sell things, you would stop any spending that wasn't required to survive, and you would take on two extra jobs. For that short nine months, you would become a saving machine. You would give up virtually anything to accomplish that $5,000 goal.

Emergency Fund

As mentioned earlier, when the unexpected happens, it's only an emergency when you don't have the cash available to take care of it. Imagine you are driving, and your car makes a funny noise. You say to yourself, "What is that?" Finally, you get an opportunity to take your car to the mechanic, and it doesn't look good. The mechanic tells you that he has identified the problem, and it can be fixed with no problem; the total cost with labor and parts $416.57. Now what? Is this an emergency or an inconvenience? I am convinced that the reason most people end up neck-deep in debt is that they don't have a proper emergency fund.

When things go wrong and the cash is not available, people use credit to get them out of the situation. This starts a continued cycle of not having cash because you have too many payments, and having too many payments because you didn't have the cash to take care of a problem. Part of any solid financial plan requires you to have a small amount of cash set aside to cover life's emergencies. Most financial planners say that you should have three to six months of your expenses set aside in a non-invested savings account. I whole-heartedly agree, but that depends on a couple things. First, do you have debt? If so, you should focus on saving only $1,000 to $1,500 as a small emergency fund. After you have this small emergency fund, you should focus all of your efforts and attention on getting out of debt.

Saving

The reason I say save only $1,000 to $1,500 and not three to six months of expenses is simple. Let's assume your expenses include all of your living expenses such as mortgage, utilities, car payment, and the minimum payments on all of your debts. Let's say that total was $4,000 per month. You will then need $12,000 in an emergency fund to have three months of expenses. However, if you saved just $1,000 and focused every extra dollar that you have available on reducing debt, and you were able to reduce your monthly expenses from $4,000 to $2,100 per month by getting rid of monthly payments, that changes things. By reducing your debts and lowering your monthly expenses to $2,100, then you would only need $6,300 in an emergency fund to cover three months of expenses.

The bottom line here is you must save money and stop using credit. Then and only then will you realize the true potential for being financially free. Having an emergency fund allows you to focus and do the things that you really and truly want to do in life. To embrace this concept you have to become a different person. You can't be the same person with the same habits and expect to get anything other than what you've got now.

What is the secret to saving?

Focused emotion: The secret to saving money is to make it a priority, and that is done only when you get some healthy anger or fear and then focus that emotion on your personal decisions. Harnessing that emotion will make you move yourself to the top of your creditor list. Until you pay yourself before everyone and everything else, you will never save money. Advertisers and the marketing community are affecting our emotions everyday and taking every dollar we have by making us see our wants as needs. It is time for this to stop!

Emotions make great slaves, but they are lousy masters.

No matter how educated or sophisticated we are, if we are not saving, we are being ruled by emotions rather than harnessing them as financial planning slaves. Whether you are saving for college tuition, a trip to the family reunion, new school clothes for little Bobby or Sally, or anything else, start saving *now*!

"To be successful you have to marry the idea of being successful and stop dating it."

— Lonnie R. Mathews

Organizing Your Financial Life

Your financial future depends on your ability to manage your money and put it to work. You may not realize it, but your assets have the potential to grow into a significant sum. I have found that people lose control of their financial lives because they tend to get sidetracked by obstacles that impede financial success. You can overcome obstacles to success if you practice sound financial management. The official definition of financial management is: the process of prioritizing the allocation of cash to support your goals. The real definition of financial management is being able to tell your money where to go and actually making it go there. Managing money is like managing children. If you don't get a handle on them at an early age, they become more and more difficult to handle later on in life.

Pretty soon you have this uncontrollable monster on your hands that you don't know how to deal with. Unfortunately, that is the relationship that most individuals have with regard to their money. Things seem to just get out of control, and you find yourself living from paycheck to paycheck, hoping that nothing major comes up. The truth is that something major always comes up. The problem with most people is that they are rarely prepared to deal with financial emergencies, and they often chose the wrong solution to handling a financial crisis. Bad financial decisions further compound any financial crisis.

The first step to building wealth is to be honest with yourself and where you are financially. Most of the time people aren't aware of where they are financially, much less what they need to do to fix their situation. The most powerful thing that anyone can do to get themselves on the right track financially is to organize their finances. Organizing your finances will set you up for success. The first thing that you want to do to get organized is to create a filling system that works for you. It is important that you keep all of your financial statements and important financial papers in one place; you should also consider opening your statements when they arrive, just to make sure the information on your account is accurate.

Now that you have opened your statements and have verified that the information is accurate store them in an organized filing system. Next, you should also develop a way to keep track of the money you spend; I personally use the financial management software *Quicken* by Intuit. I like this system because it allows me to download my banking information regularly, and I am then able to organize the information to suit my needs. You don't have to use this method, but it is important that you find a system that works for you. Several free online tools are available, such as www.mint.com. The point is to find something that helps you get organized. The next thing that I usually recommend is to create a bill payment system. By creating this system, you will get a sense of who you owe and when they need to be paid. There are probably several ways to create a bill payment schedule; I recommend the simplest way that works for you. I have created a spreadsheet with five columns. The first column is labeled "name." This column lists the name of all of your vendors or the people you pay on a monthly basis.

The next four columns are labeled for the weeks of the month, i.e. 1st thru 7th, 8th thru 15th etcetera. Each column represents the weeks in the month. When you go down the list of vendors, you will put an X or check in the column of the week of the month that represents when the payment is due for each vendor. For example, in the name column, you will put the name of your power company. Then look at your old power bill and find when the bill is due each month. If your bill is due on the 10th of each month, you will put a check or better yet, write the 10th in the second column.

By creating a system such as this one, you will get a sense of organization in your financial life, and you can use this information to help you determine which bill is due, based on when you expect to get paid each pay period. This information will also be useful later in this book when I discuss the process of developing a budget that works for you. Organized finances will help you to make better decisions about your money. Many of us believe that a higher income ensures financial stability. Unfortunately, poor spending habits carry over, regardless of salary. Being organized with your financial affairs requires proper planning, discipline, and sometimes, significant changes to your everyday life.

Goals

To truly be successful at anything in life, you have to set goals. By setting financial goals, you give yourself a road map to success. Author Mark McCormack speaks of a study done in 1979 in his book, *what they don't teach you in Harvard Business School.* In this study, the students of the 1979 MBA class were asked upon graduation, "Have you set clear written goals for your future and made plans to accomplish them?" According to the study, only 3 percent of the students responding said they had. Another 13 percent had goals, but had not written them down, and the remaining 84 percent had no goals set at all. Fast forward ten years, and those same individuals were found and interviewed, and as you can imagine, the results were predictable at best.

The individuals who had goals, but had not written them down earned on average two times as much as did the individuals with no goals at all. But the really amazing part is that the 3 percent with a clear set of written goals and a written plan for accomplishing those goals earned on average ten times as much as the rest of the 97 percent of the class.

A goal not written down is nothing more than a dream.

When it comes to goals, there are certain things that have to happen to accomplish any goal. First, you have to understand the importance of having goals. Most individuals who are successful in their chosen profession, regardless of what that profession is, have goals. Having goals is the one thing that sets successful people apart from the not-so-successful people. So now is the time, and today is the day that you need to set some goals. When we go through life without goals, it is like getting in your car and just driving with no particular destination in mind. What normally happens if you do this long enough is that you will wake up one day and realize that you are in a place where you do not want to be? Let's face it. No one ever sets out to be a financial failure. It's the lack of goals and direction that normally gets them there.

Here's what you should do. Grab a pen, a sheet of paper, and spend some time thinking about where you would like to be financially. Next, think of three financial goals that you would like to accomplish—three things that if completed would change your life for the better. As you are doing this, categorize these three goals into different time periods. Goals should fall into three categories. You should have a short-term or immediate goal; this is something that you can accomplish in one year or less. The next goal should be a mid-term goal. This is something that you can and should accomplish anytime from one year to three years from now. Finally, you should set a long-term goal. This is anything that you want to accomplish anytime, three years or beyond.

1. _____
2. _____
3. _____

Of course, you can have more than one goal in each category. In fact, you can have as many goals as you can actually accomplish within each category. Be careful not to create so many goals that you can't accomplish them all. Now that you have your goals *written*, evaluate each goal to make sure that it is a S.M.A.R.T goal. When I say *smart*, I don't mean intelligent, but the goals should be:

S	=	Specific
M	=	Measurable
A	=	Attainable
R	=	Realistic
T	=	Time bound

By sticking to this formula, you are ensuring that you have what it takes to actually accomplish these goals. It is also important to understand during this goal-setting process, that this may be new to you, and it will take some getting used to the idea of setting and working toward a goal. That is why it is important for you to write your goals down and make several copies. Keep them in places where you can see them often. I personally keep a copy in my office at home, a copy in my office at work, and a copy in my briefcase. That way I am constantly reminded of my goals. Writing goals helps me keep focused on what I am supposed to be doing. You may be asking, "Why go to so much trouble in setting goals? Why can't I just set some goals? Why do they need to be SMART goals?" Here's why you need SMART goals.

Specific

Goals should be straight forward and to the point. Each goal should emphasize exactly what you what to happen in the future. You want to use these goals to guide your behavior to a particular point in the future. Your goal should be a simple as: what, why, and how. To set a goal to be rich is too vague. *To set a goal to save $2,000 to create a cushion for a financial emergency is an example of a specific goal.*

Measurable

If you can't measure your goals, how can you honestly expect to manage these goals, much less accomplish them? The key here is to choose a goal on which you can track your progress. You want to choose something for which you can actually see the results of progress and get a sense of accomplishment as you are working toward your goal. When you have measurable goals it allows you to stay on track as you reach specific milestones. By reaching small milestones in the process of working toward a goal, you are encouraged to continue your efforts.

Attainable

While it is important to set goals that you can obtain, you should set goals that will stretch you a little. In other words, you don't want to set a goal that you know without a doubt you can complete, but you also don't want to set goals that you know you don't have the ability to achieve without extraordinary stress, or perhaps not at all. In other words, your goals should be "do-able." At best, a goal should be something that you can do, but just haven't gotten around to doing. In other words, you have everything you need to accomplish this goal, but haven't done it yet. The feelings of success that you will get by obtaining these goals will help motivate you to continue to stretch yourself.

Realistic

Realistic goals don't mean they should be super easy. They should be something that you really want to accomplish and will take you closer to where you want to be. I remember talking to a lady after doing one of my financial seminars, and she was excited about the information she had received, and she wanted to do better financially. In her excitement, she said that her goal was to save $10,000 next year. I thought to myself, *Wow! That is a great goal.* So I asked her, "How much did you save last year?" Her response was "Nothing." That is an example of a goal that is not very realistic, in my opinion. If a person didn't save any money last year, how can she expect to start saving $833.33 per month to have $10,000 in savings within a year?

Timely

The last thing that is an absolute must when it comes to goals is they must be measurable by a specific time period. By setting a timeframe to your goals, you are putting an automatic endpoint to the goal. That way the goal doesn't linger on forever. By putting a time on your goals, you have a clear target to work towards. So even though you have your goals broken down into categories such as short-term, mid-term, and long-term, you should also set a specific date within those categories. Remember, without a time limit there is no urgency so *start now!*

Even more important than setting goals is actually achieving them. One way to achieve your goals is to have a system of accountability to keep you on track. If you are married, and both you and your spouse sit down and establish common goals, then it will be easy to keep each other accountable. Another way to get that accountability is to tell others about your goals. In other words, don't keep your goals to yourself. When I first decided to write this book, I wanted to have these words on paper a lot sooner. I remember running into a friend who I had previously told that I was finishing my next book. One of the first things my friend asked me was how was the book coming, and was I finished? Imagine how I felt, having to say that I wasn't. That simple meeting was enough to motivate me to continue writing and ultimately finish this book.

The difference between living and existing is having goals.

In the end, goals give you a sense of purpose. Goals give you a sense of why you even get out of bed in the morning. *Webster* defines *living* as, "active or thriving; having life, vigorous and strong," as compared to *existing*, which is defined as, "having the basic needs met, such as food and shelter." When you have goals you get a sense of being, you have a feeling of trying to get things done.

"Become a student of change. It is the only thing that will remain constant."

— Anthony J. D'Angelo

Budget Smudget

In his book, *Rich Dad Poor Dad*, author Robert Kiyasaki wrote, "With each dollar that enters your hand you and only you have the power to determine your destiny. Spend it foolishly, you choose to be poor. Spend it on liabilities, you join the middle class. Invest it in your mind and learn how to acquire assets, and you will be choosing wealth as your goal and your future." As I am writing this chapter, these words echo in my mind, because when most people hear the word *budget*, they cringe. I will admit that before I started the process of getting where I wanted to be financially, I didn't budget my income either. When I looked up the word in the dictionary, here is what I found.

Budg-et: noun—*an estimate, often itemized, of expected income and expense for a given period in the future.*

I like to think of a budget as telling your money where to go and making it go there. The most difficult part of budgeting is following through. Just about anyone with an 8th grade education can figure out how to develop a budget; the math part isn't very difficult. It's actually making it happen that makes the difference. It's about conquering the desire to spend money on things that really aren't necessary, it's about conquering you. I often say during seminars that personal finance is only 20 percent head knowledge and 80 percent personal. For most people the thought of having to budget their income seems overwhelming. Budgeting in its simplest form is the process of allocating your income to meet certain obligations or predetermined goals. Budgeting is about setting limits on where you spend your money; it's about determining where you want to be financially and then purposely directing your income there.

Most people's financial lives are just like the individual in the first chapter; most people live with controlled chaos when it comes to their financial lives. If you are one of those individuals who has never given any thought as to how you spend your income—if payday comes and you don't have a predetermined plan on how you are going to spend your paycheck—now is the time to stop. Getting ahead financially requires you to create new habits that will allow you to change your financial picture. Changing your financial picture is about creating habits that will allow you to get there. It's like getting into great physical shape. First you will stop doing the things that contribute to your poor physical condition, and then you will have to start doing the things that will get you into good physical shape.

Why should I use a budget?

There are several reasons why a family should start and follow a monthly budget. In today's fast-moving world, it's all too easy to access your money through checking accounts and ATM/check cards. Therefore, it is easy to lose track of how much you are really spending.

We also live in a society that has taught us to "buy now, pay later." This method has caused some consumers to overspend and become knee-deep in debt.

Consumers need to take control of their spending and realize that their financial situation can improve with proper budgeting. Unless you are actually tracking your money, it's probably not going where you really need and want it to go. One of the main goals of budgeting is to get a handle on your money and to make sure your monthly expenses do not exceed your monthly take-home income.

A budget is one of the most important tools in managing your personal finances. The best way to develop a budget is to use some type of money management software. However, you can simply use a note pad and pencil, and I will show you how to do it in the next few pages. When you develop a budget, make sure that it is a livable one. In other words, don't set amounts you need for food and other necessities very low, just so you can pay debt off faster. By livable, I mean a budget you can realistically stick to based on your current spending habits.

How can I control my spending?

First, you need to control the emotions and impulses that stimulate your desire to spend money. Second, you should keep close track of what you spend, so you can stretch your dollars as far as they can go, whether it's buying food, clothes, or paying monthly household bills. Ask yourself, "What can I realistically do without?" In addition, you should be able to cut back on personal care, hobbies, and entertainment.

The most common and simple way to track your spending is to take a piece of paper (or use a computer) and write down all your monthly living expenses and other monthly bills. Based on your monthly net income, you should set "target amounts" per expense (such as $200 for food, $100 for entertainment, etc.). By setting target amounts, you can monitor where you are overspending each month. Overspending leads to financial problems. You can start by listing all of your fixed expenses each month (such as housing, auto, insurance, food, etc.), as well as non-fixed monthly expenses (entertainment, personal care, auto repairs, medical, travel, etc.).

The best way to predict your non-fixed monthly expenses is to look at your check register or bank statements for the past three months. This will give you a rough idea as to where to set target amounts for non-fixed expenses. Also add in quarterly, semi-annual, and annual expenses, such as insurance premiums, property taxes, and car registration.

Household expenses are categorized into essential and discretionary. Because many expenses are variable, such as utilities and groceries, it is important to average these expenses. Other expenses are periodic (such as insurance or vehicle registration). Entertainment and kid's activities are two areas that people don't plan and budget for. Going out to dinner, going to the movies or taking kids to an amusement park is easy, knowing that you can withdraw money using your ATM card. Most people do things on the spur of the moment, with no idea as to how it could affect their cash flow. Entertainment can be budgeted for the family by allocating a target amount (such as $200) each month.

There are four elements to successful a budget.

It must be written

If you don't write it down, then it's not a budget; it's just that simple! It really doesn't matter what you write it on, or how you keep track of it; just write it down! It is often the man in a relationship who thinks that he is capable of keeping the budget details in his head. No matter how good you are with numbers, a budget must be in writing.

It must be done together

If you live alone, this step does not apply to you. But assuming that you are sharing the responsibility of making ends meet with a spouse, son, daughter, cousin, aunt, uncle, stepson, stepdaughter, or a roommate, then you both must be on the same page and in agreement as to how the money will be spent. A chain is only as strong as its weakest link. The key is to make spending decisions together and on purpose.

It must be completed before the month begins

A true budget is a spending plan for the future. This is not to be confused with a spending record, which is merely a summary of how much was spent in the past. Once the plan is established, there must be a method to track its progress. This is a critical step. Most people don't pre-plan how they are going to spend their income. It is usually done after the fact or after some crisis has happened, and then they are forced to pre-plan how they are going to spend their income.

It must be easy

Simply put, establish a spending plan, track the plan, spend less than you make, and do it again the next month. When you prepare a household budget, you can predict monthly net income and monthly living expenses. Understanding your cash flow will help you see how much "disposable net income" you have left over each month for savings, vacations, and etcetera. The bottom line is that the process of budgeting should not add complication to your life. A budget is supposed to make life easier.

On paper, on purpose

From this point on, forget everything that you have heard or know about budgeting. The reason that most people don't budget is because they make it too complicated. Budgeting is about changing your habits to support the life style you want to have. It's not about living so strictly that you take the joy out of life. I discovered a simple approach to budgeting that doesn't' require a lot. Before we get started, there are several tools that you will need in order to budget successfully. The tools you will need are a pencil with an eraser, a note pad, and a calculator—and that's it. Now that you have the tools, here is what you should do. The first thing you want to do is clear your mind of everything that you have ever known about budgeting. Next, prepare to be persistent.

The process is not going to get better over night. Let's face it. You didn't develop bad habits over night. I usually tell people that it will take ninety days for you to get the hang of things.

The first few times you try this, you will forget to include a couple of things. If you do forget something, don't worry about it. Just rework your budget. Eventually, you will get the hang of it.

Instead of just waiting until payday to start paying bills and spending money, the key to my technique is to spend your entire paycheck on paper and on purpose before payday. Here's what I mean. Let's say that your payday is Friday of next week. On Wednesday of next week, take some time, gather your bills, and determine which ones are due between this coming payday and the next, and which ones can wait until after the next time you get paid. At the top of the note pad, in the far left hand corner, write the date that you get paid. Next, go down a couple of lines, and in the middle of the page, write the amount you bring home that appears on your paycheck stub. From here, look at the bills that you know you have to pay this payday, and begin listing them below the amount of your bring-home pay. After listing the bills that you have to pay this payday, total them up and subtract them from your bring-home pay.

From here you will discover one of two things. After subtracting the most essential bills and the bills with a fixed payment, you will notice that you will have either a surplus or a deficit. If you have a deficit, then you are having some very serious financial issues that need immediate attention. What this is saying is that you are overspending to maintain your current standard of living. The only way you can sustain this lifestyle is to finance the difference. Usually you are using credit cards to make up the difference. You can only use credit to subsidize your lifestyle for so long before you are not able to get more credit. If you find yourself in this position, you should seek financial counseling right away.

The other thing that you may find after paying your fixed and essential bills is that you have a surplus. Having a surplus is a good thing; this means that you have money left over each month. The next thing is to find out what is happening to that surplus every month. If you are like most people, you honestly don't know. That is where my budgeting technique comes in handy. If you have a surplus, the next thing that you want to do is to first figure out how much will be left. Then sit down and think about what you want to spend this money on. As you are doing this, please be honest with yourself. If you can look at your bank statement and can see that you spend $200 eating out every month, you will either make the decision to not eat out as much or just go ahead and write down that you will spend $200 dollars eating out this month.

What you shouldn't do is to pretend that somehow this month you aren't going to eat out. The point of this is to pre-spend your entire pay check on paper and on purpose before you get your money. By doing this, you will get a sense of control over where your money is going each month. You may not make drastic changes right away, but by doing this every time you get paid, you will ultimately make the decision to not spend as much eating out every month.

The real challenge to this technique is to follow through with your planned spending. This is the tough part for the average adult. It just seems that life happens and things come up that you had not planned on. If this happens, don't worry or panic. You will simply have to look at your planned budget and decide which areas you are going to cut. Once you have made the decision, go ahead; make the changes and continue forward.

The beauty of this technique is that it does not require you to make drastic changes that you probably won't continue doing anyway. The idea is that over time you will see where your money is going each and every pay period and decide to permanently change the way you do things. To truly change, it must be a permanent change. If you don't, however, do this simple, yet effective budgeting technique, you will forever ask yourself where your money is going. By not doing this, you are undoubtedly going to spend the extra money in your budget on something trivial and useless.

The real trick to budgeting is to somehow become cognizant of where your money is going and how much you are spending on a regular basis. I have been doing this for so long that it is now second nature to me. I am constantly doing a mental check to track how much money I am spending on any given day. I am not saying that you have to be this anal about your money, but not keeping track at all is not working either. The trick is to find a healthy balance between spending unconsciously and recklessly spending away every dime that you make, and being a super tightwad. This technique is designed to help you to stop wondering why you can't ever seem to save, why you can't ever seem to get ahead financially, why you are no better off now than your were five years ago even though you make more money than you did then.

What is a Percentage Guideline Budget?

Each year the US Census Bureau conducts The Consumer Expenditure Survey (CE). This survey provides a snapshot of the U.S. Economy and the spending habits of American citizens from various parts of the country. While the information collected in this survey is largely used by policymakers to assess the impact of policy changes on the spending patterns to predict inflation, I have found that it has another very practical purpose.

Field representatives from the census bureau gather information about how much many American households spend for several items, such as clothing, housing, transportation health care, and groceries. This data is gathered from a sample of households all across the United States. To collect this information, over 43,000 households are interviewed every three months over a fifteen month period regarding expenditures on large items occurring on a regular basis, such as rent and utilities. Then throughout the year, another 9,300 households are asked to keep two consecutive one-week diaries of their smaller, more frequent purchases, such as candy bars and vending machine purchases.

"What is the practical purpose of this?" you might ask. Well, I have figured out a way to use this information for a personal use, and that use is called the percentage guideline budget. The percentage guideline budget is where you look at the different categories from the survey as a percentage of your annual income. You can also think of a guideline budget as a family-spending plan divided into percentages to help determine the proper balance for each category of your budget. The main use of a guideline budget is to find out the areas that may need some attention or to identify an area that could be causing financial stress in your life.

The following guideline budget is developed as a standard to compare your current spending against and to achieve a healthy financial lifestyle. After putting together a guideline budget, you may reconsider future financial decisions. For example, you may find that you are spending too much on cars, and decide that in the future, you will change your situation. Although the percentages are not absolute, they can serve as a guide to help you put things into perspective. If for some reason, you find yourself out of balance, don't panic. It's not the end of the world. It just means that you have some tough decisions to make regarding your future spending. The chart on the next page shows the spending by category from the most recent Consumer Expenditure survey.

Percentage Guide

Gross Income	$25,000	$35,000	$45,000	$55,000	$85,000	$125,000
Giving	2,500	3,500	4,500	5,500	8,500	12,500
Taxes (1)	3,250	6,650	9,000	11,550	18,000	30,000
Net Spendable Income	**$19,250**	**$24,850**	**$31,500**	**$37,950**	**$58,500**	**$82,500**
Housing	38%	36%	32%	31%	30%	30%
Food	14%	11%	11%	11%	11%	11%
Transportation	16%	16%	17%	18%	15%	15%
Insurance	5%	5%	5%	5%	5%	5%
Debts	4%	5%	5%	5%	5%	5%
Entertainment/ Recreation	4%	5%	6%	6%	7%	8%
Clothing	3%	3%	5%	5%	5%	7%
Savings	5%	5%	5%	5%	5%	5%
Medical / Dental	4%	4%	4%	4%	4%	4%
Miscellaneous	4%	5%	5%	5%	5%	5%
Investments (2)	3%	5%	5%	5%	8%	5%
If you have school/child care expenses, these percentages must be deducted from other categories						
School / Child Care	8%	6%	5%	5%	5%	5%
TOTAL	**100%**	**100%**	**100%**	**100%**	**100%**	**100%**

1 The tax category includes taxes for Social Security and a small amount for state taxes.
To be accurate you will need to calculate your actual taxes, due to the frequent changes in the taxe code

2 This is used to fund long-term goals such as education or retirement

Things to Consider

There are several things to consider in the chart above. First, notice that the chart is broken down by income ranges. You should find where your income falls within the ranges of gross income. Notice that after you take into consideration subtracting a small amount for giving to your favorite charity and federal income taxes, you have what's call the net spendable income. If you have to pay state taxes, your NSI may be a little lower. Either way, that is all you have to spend.

After looking at the chart above, go ahead and calculate

what your percentages are for the given areas and match them to the chart. By doing this, you will see how your current budget and current lifestyle stack up against the national averages. One of the first things that you should notice is that housing should range anywhere from 30 to 38 percent of your NSI. Please take note that housing includes all the things related to having a home and not just the house payment. Housing actually includes the payment, taxes, insurance, and utilities. Most financial experts will tell you that your payment should not be more than twenty-five percent of your bring-home pay.

In all the years that I have counseled individuals, the one area that most individuals are out of line in is the automobile or transportation category. Notice that the average family spends anywhere from 15 to 20 percent on transportation costs. Again, notice that this includes the automobile payment, insurance, fuel, and maintenance costs for the year. Most people find this very shocking, and find that they are in way over their head when it comes to automobiles.

When you look at your budget from an annual perspective, it's like being in an airplane and flying over your house. When you fly over your house, you tend to see things a little differently. You tend to notice things that you didn't notice before. I didn't realize how much of my annual income I was spending on my favorite indulgence—*gourmet coffee.*

I had developed the insane habit of stopping every morning and getting a hot cup of coffee at the local coffee bar on my way out. Sometimes I would even get up on Saturday morning and go and enjoy a cup of coffee. It wasn't until I had just finished fussing about our budget to my wife that she pointed out to me what I was doing. My wife asked me how much I spent on coffee every year. I have to admit that I hadn't thought much about it, and then I ran the numbers. I was spending on average $5 per day for coffee. If you multiply that times five days a week on average, and sometimes six days, I was spending no less than $25 per week on coffee. In a year's time, I would spend over $1,300 per year on coffee.

Now it's your turn. What's your indulgement and how much is it costing you? Then ask yourself how much of your annual income is that, and what am I giving up for this indulgence? Once I discovered what my indulgence was costing me, I no longer drink gourmet coffee every day. Now I only drink it on special occasions.

"Debt: An ingenious substitute for the chain and whip of the slave driver."

— Ambrose Bierce

"Debt is like any other trap, easy enough to get into, but hard enough to get out of. "

— Henry Wheeler Shaw

Controlling Debt

In his book, *The Greatest Salesman in the World*, inspirational author Og Mandino stated, "I have surrendered my free will to the years of accumulated habits, and the past deeds of my life have charted a course that now threatens to imprison my future." If you are one of those people who think that life will get better without any effort to change, you are engaging self-delusion. To escape the clutches of debt, you must first take a new look at the word interest. With regard to money, you are either paying interest or earning it. Your financial success or failure in life is determined by whether you earn more interest than you pay. You see, owing money to others obligates you to give them your hard earned dollars, and in a lot of cases you must give it to them even before you save any for yourself.

It easy to get caught up in living life, and then start purchasing things on credit without thinking. Then you find yourself burdened with debt from your past decisions. Today is the day you take back control of your financial life; you must rid yourself of the power of debt and discover a new you. It is debt that stands guard in the doorway leading to your fortune, your future, and your legacy; debt must be cast aside.

Is Debt a Problem in Your Life?

According to recent headlines, consumer debt in America is over a trillion dollars. When surveyed, more than half of all credit cardholders say they don't pay their cards off each month and carry an average balance of around $2,000. It's obvious that debt has gotten out of hand. Most individuals don't set out to get themselves in to debt; it just happens. Getting into debt is easy. All you have to do is live your life and not be aware of where you are financially. In other words, when you don't live on a budget, you really aren't aware of where you are financially, and life just happens. While there are probably several obstacles to building real wealth, the biggest reason why people don't build wealth is the misuse of debt.

The first step in the journey to financial freedom requires you to come to the realization that you are in debt.

In other words, you have to face your demons. By facing your demons, you come to the point where you realize that you have debt, and in a lot of cases, you don't really know how much debt you have.

Before we get started on this journey, the first thing that you must do is to make the commitment to *not* use debt anymore. The only way not to accumulate additional debt is to cut up existing credit cards and pay for everything with cash, check, or debit card at the time of purchase. But, before performing plastic surgery, all of your surplus dollars should be directed toward building a small emergency fund to handle any unplanned expenses. A good start would be a minimum of $1,000 to $1,500, depending on your income and ability to raise cash. For some people, this may sound counter-intuitive.

"Why should I save before paying off debt?" If you don't save first, you're not going to be able to deal with unexpected expenses. Do not tell yourself that you can keep a credit card for emergencies. Destroy your credit cards; save cash for emergencies. After you've stopped using credit, and after you've saved an emergency fund, then attack your existing debt. Attack your debt with vigor by throwing whatever you can at it.

What follows is a four step process to getting completely out of debt. There are a lot of ways to get out of debt, so whatever way you find that works for you, go with that. The method that I have created comes from trying different things until I found something that worked for me and my family and I want to share it with you. If you are one of those individuals who is in a place where you don't want to be financially, then give this a try. Remember don't be afraid to rework things until you find something that works!

Step 1. Figure out how much you owe, to whom, and on what terms.

Often times when you are in debt, you feel overwhelmed and don't want to deal with the situation. Most people don't have a clear idea of the extent to which they are in debt. Gather your bills, and make a simple list or spreadsheet of all the debts you have. Write down all the pertinent facts, including name of the creditor, your total balance, your minimum monthly payment, and your interest rate.

As a follow-up to step one on a separate sheet of paper, or again, on a spreadsheet, write the names of your creditors. In a column next to their names, list the total amount owed. In a second column, list the minimum monthly payment. The next step requires you to clear your mind of everything you have ever heard about paying off debt. It is time to do something different. It has been said, "The definition of insanity is doing the same thing over and over again, and expecting a different result." If you have been going through life with the same habits, how can you expect something different to happen unless you change?

Step 2. Calculate your debt payoff priority.

To calculate your debt payoff priority, take the total amount you owe each creditor and divide that amount by the minimum payment. This in of itself means nothing, but what this number represents is roughly how many months it is going to take to pay this particular debt off just by making the minimum payments.

Example: *you have a $700 balance on a credit card, and the minimum payment is $50. If you divide 700 by 50, you will get an answer of 14.*

This number says that you have approximately fourteen months to pay this balance by making just the minimum payments. In reality, if you factor in the average interest rate of 14.1 percent, it would take you sixteen months to pay the balance. This number is known as the payoff priority. You should repeat this process for all your creditors. Now that you have determined the payoff priority for each creditor, these numbers indicate which debt you should pay off first. The creditor with the lowest number would be the first debt to be paid off.

What this process really reveals is that if all else remains the same, and you continued to make minimum payments, the creditor with the lowest payoff priority would be the first debt to be paid off. Interest rate is not the issue at this point; our goal here is to accelerate the date which this debt will be paid off by using your surplus. Even if your surplus is a nominal amount, by adding only $100 extra to each minimum payment, it would take several months off the time to pay the balance.

Step 3. Cut your lifestyle your spending.

By now you should know the importance of budgeting your income. By budgeting, you tell your money where to go, and not the other way around. Take a good look at your monthly spending and figure out where you can make some cuts. Don't say, "There is nothing to cut." If you say that, either you haven't done a budget in a while, or you are living in some fantasy world where you think everything that you are spending your money on is a necessity.

The truth is that there is probably more fluff in your budget that you think. I know for a fact that my cable and internet bill is $120 per month (ouch). Sometimes you have to make the tough choices in life. Either I am willing to cut out cable and internet for a little while or I am okay being in debt. No one can make the choice except you. You have to decide that today is the day that you will do something different; today is the day that you will change your life forever.

Step 4. Attack! (and stick to the plan)

Now that you have listed your debts, determine which one has the lowest payoff priority, and you have found extra money in your budget; even if it means that you need to get that dreaded second job (only for a little while), you are ready to begin. Before we take the next step, let me mention a couple things. First, if you are like most people and you have listed your debts, you may notice that you have a lot of small balances that are below $500. Before implementing this strategy, take any extra money and get those accounts out of the way. For instance, list anything less than $1,000 from the smallest to the largest, and take the surplus money in your budget and any other money that you can pull together, and pay off these smaller debts.

Now that you have the smaller ones done, you will have a sense of accomplishment. Take that momentum and continue to attack. The next thing you want to do is to continue to pay the minimum payment on all of your accounts. Nothing more and nothing less just the minimum.

Then go back to the debt payoff priority list and find the account with the lowest payoff priority number. Now that you have cleared up some smaller debts, you should have a little extra money to work with. Starting with the lowest payoff priority balance, make the minimum payment plus any extra money you can put towards it, while continuing to make the minimum on everything else. You will continue this process until that debt is paid off.

Once you have paid off one balance, take the payments that you were making and roll that payment to the next debt on the payoff priority list. You should continue this process until all the debts are gone. The truth is that most people could be debt free in three to five years. The problem is most people have not tried.

Once you realize what a powerful mathematical tool this is, finding additional money to reduce your debt will not be a problem. Imagine debt that would normally take a lifetime to pay back being gone in just a few months. Remember, the month after a debt is eliminated; you take that minimum payment plus your accelerator and add it to the next debt. This process may go against everything that you may have been taught about money, but it works. By the time you get to other larger payments such as a vehicle, or even your mortgage, your accelerator will be large. Assuming you follow this payoff priority method, you will soon find yourself in the position to say "good-bye" to debt forever.

Getting into debt is easy. Just buy a few things that you can't afford to pay for in cash, and don't think about how many payments you are going to have to make before it's paid off completely. Getting into debt is fun; all it takes is going out for a dinner and a movie once or twice, you know, just to take your mind off the fact that you never have any money to go out with. Now that your eyes are open to the horror of "easy monthly payments," the good news is that there is hope. You can get out of debt. Everybody has their own theory when it comes to getting out of debt. Getting out of debt takes discipline, planning, and sometimes significant changes to your spending habits.

In the following example, Figure 1 illustrates the debt payoff priority of a typical family with various types of debts.

Name of debt	Total Balance	Minimum Payment	Divisor	Pay-off Priority	Margin Roll-Up	Pay-Off Months
1	2	3	4	5	6	7
Mortgage	$90,000	$593	151.8	7	$2,068	43.5
Visa	$3,797	$76	50.0	6	$1,475	2.6
MasterCard	$4,008	$81	49.5	5	$1,399	2.9
Home Equity Loan	$3,186	$75	42.5	4	$1,318	2.4
Finger Furniture	$2,348	$117	20.0	3	$1,243	1.9
Car Payment #2	$8,754	$483	18.1	2	$1,126	7.8
Car Payment #1	$5,365	$393	13.7	1	$643	8.4
TOTAL	$117,458	$1,818				
Accelerator					$250	
Total monthy payment					$1,818	

Figure 1.

In our example, this couple has $117,458 total debt. If this couple would simply get committed to getting debt out of their lives forever and making an effort to never use debt again, they could use the priority payoff method and add an accelerator of $250, which would make this family debt free in five years and ten months. Debt has a definite payoff date; the problem comes when we keep adding to the debt. When we add additional debt, we continually set the payoff date back.

Credit Card \ kred' et Kard \ n.: 1. A means for buying something you don't need, at a price you can't afford, with money you don't have, usually to impress people you don't like.

Why Credit?

Credit cards make it convenient in our everyday lives to purchase almost everything jewelry, computers, clothes, groceries, and etcetera. Some credit cards are accepted worldwide, while others are good for particular stores. Either way, the concept is the same. The concept is that when you use a credit card, you are spending future dollars today. Each time you take a "cash advance" on your credit card or purchase an item with your credit card, you're actually signing a contract between yourself and the credit card issuer for a loan. That means you agree to repay the principal loan plus interest on the unpaid balance. The use of credit is not free; for most people credit is very expensive. If you use credit now, it means that you are spending money that you will earn in the future. That means that you will have to do without things that you need and want later.

Look at the following example: Let's say you are offered a credit card with a limit of $1,000. The annual percentage rate (APR) is 19.8%. You accept the terms, and begin to use your card to purchase things such as clothes, food, gas, and gifts for your friends and family. You even purchase a CD player and some CDs on sale.

Soon you reach your limit of $1,000, but your minimum payment is only $20 per month. As long as you make this small payment each month, the credit card company will be happy. Doesn't that sound like a great deal? It is for the credit card company, but for you, no! Let's take a closer look at your account. Remember, your balance is $1,000, and you make the minimum payments of $20 per month. By just making the minimum payments each month, it will take 107 months to pay off this card. That's almost nine years! By then the clothes will be out of style, the food and gas will be gone, the gifts will be forgotten, and the CDs might be obsolete (remember records).

The total interest paid on the card will be $1,129.91. That's more than the original balance. If this still sounds like a good deal to you, keep in mind that this example assumes that you never charge on this card again after the original $1,000. If you use the card again during the pay-off time, it will take you more than nine years to repay, and will cost you even more in interest.

Credit: Past and Present

The credit card is a relatively new phenomenon; in fact, the first credit card was created in 1959 by Bank of America. Since then, Americans have managed to rack up over one trillion dollars in credit card debt. Bank of America began issuing the BankAmericard in California. It was the first universal credit card with widespread merchant acceptance. In 1966, a group of fourteen US banks formed Interlink, a new bankcard processing association with the ability to exchange information on credit card transactions.

In 1967, four California banks formed the Western States Bankcard Association and introduced the Master-Charge program (which was later renamed MasterCard in 1979) to compete with the BankAmericard (later renamed Visa in 1976) program. VISA and MasterCard are organizations that both process credit cards through member banks and set and maintain the rules for processing. Today both Visa and MasterCard process tens of thousands transactions every day. So what does that translate to in today's terms? As of the writing of this book, here's what it looks like. At the end of 2008, Americans' credit card debt reached $972.73 billion. That number includes both general purpose credit cards and private-label credit cards that aren't owned by a bank. Average credit card debt per household was $8,329, and the average outstanding credit card debt for households that have a credit card was $10,679.

Now what?

What do employers, potential landlords, insurance companies, and utility companies have in common? They are all part of a growing trend in America. They all check your credit score prior to quoting you a price. Now you would expect companies that lend consumers money to check your credit, but insurance companies? To most companies your credit score is an indicator of your character; I have personally struggled with that concept for the past few years. On the one hand, a business owner or anyone that is going to enter into a financial relationship with someone should be concerned about a person's character. I think it is important to know if a person has a habit of entering into financial obligations and not following through on those obligations. Your credit score in a lot of circumstances is the best indicator; it basically shows how you have treated others in the past with regard to your payment history, and how you have managed your financial affairs. If you were constantly late in making payments, your score will reflect it. If you didn't honor your financial obligations, your score will reflect it. If you have too much credit, your score will reflect it. However, sometimes individuals go through difficult times that prevent them from meeting all of their obligations, and this happens more often than not. In that instance, I think the credit score doesn't accurately reflect a person's character—at least not at that given moment. One of the biggest distractions for employees is financial problems; studies have shown that employers lose on average as much as $7,000 per year per employee in lost productivity, because of employees having financial problems. Most employers are now checking your credit as part of a pre-employment background check. When you fill out that paper work to get a new job, you are also giving them permission to check your credit. This information is important to employers for various reasons. Number one, companies are interested in the types of employees they have. This also gives them the opportunity to know what kind of employee you will be.

I remember getting my first job at a bank after graduating from college. One day after working there for about three months, I received a call from human resources. I was told that I had a tax lien (which I didn't know about), and that I needed to get that fixed if I wanted to stay employed. Wow! Imagine not getting, or worse, losing a job because of bad credit. Well, it can happen. Maintaining a good credit history is very important in the credit driven society that we currently live in.

Where do I start?

When it comes to your credit, the first place to start is to get an idea of where you are with regard to your credit. This means that you will have to get a copy of your most recent credit report; most people that I talk to haven't seen a copy of their credit report since Bill Clinton was in office. A lot of people assume they have bad credit and just don't want to check it. In a lot of cases that is true, but either way, you need to know what potential lenders and employers will be looking at when they check your credit. By checking your credit, you are in the beginning stages of fixing any potential problems that you might have.

On December 4, 2003, the Fair and Accurate Credit Transactions Act of 2003 (FACTA) was signed into law by President George W. Bush. The act allows consumers to request and obtain a free credit report once every twelve months from each of the three nationwide consumer credit reporting companies (Equifax, Experian and TransUnion). In cooperation with the Federal Trade Commission, the three major credit reporting agencies set up a Web site to provide free access to annual credit reports. The act also contains provisions to help reduce identity theft, such as the ability for individuals to place alerts on their credit histories if identity theft is suspected, or if deploying overseas in the military, thereby making fraudulent applications for credit more difficult. Further, it requires secure disposal of consumer information.

If you haven't checked your credit in a while, I urge you to go right now and get a copy of your report from all three reporting agencies. The law has made it easy to do so. All you have to do is go to www.annualcreditreport.com and get a free copy. Once you get a copy, take some time to look over each report, checking for the accuracy of each item. If there are any discrepancies, you have the right to have those items removed or proven to be accurate by the reporting company.

As you are pulling your credit report, you will also have

the option to purchase your credit score. The law only allows you to get your report for free; the score in most cases will cost you $7 or $8, depending on the reporting agency. You will have to purchase a score from each agency, because they all have their own version of your score. In the next few pages of this chapter, I will attempt to explain to you how to improve and maintain a good credit score. By taking this step, you are finally facing your financial situation. Remember that nothing is permanent, and nothing happens without making a decision to change. If you change the present, you will ultimately change the future. It's up to you!

What is bad credit anyway?

You are considered to have bad credit when your credit score is low in comparison to the general population. By using key information from your credit report, your credit score can be calculated. Your score is calculated by a mathematical equation that evaluates several pieces of information from your credit report.

By comparing this information to the patterns in hundreds of thousands of past credit reports, the score identifies your level of future credit risk. While there are several credit scoring models that out there, the most common one used by lenders is the FICO score created by Fair Isaac Corp. Your FICO score ranges from 300 to 850. The higher your score, the better. Right now the median FICO score in the United States is 723.

In order for a FICO® score to be calculated, your credit report must contain at least one account that has been open for six months or greater. In addition, the report must contain at least one account that has been updated in the past six months. This ensures that there is enough information and enough recent information in your report on which to base a score. FICO scores are provided to lenders by the three major credit reporting agencies: Equifax, Experian and TransUnion. So you actually have three different scores—one from each of three different reporting agencies.

About FICO scores

FICO scores provide the best guide to future risk based solely on credit report data. The higher the score, the lower the risk. But no score says whether a specific individual will be a "good" or "bad" customer. While most lenders do check your credit score, the actual decision to lend will also take into consideration other factors. Each lender has its own strategy, including the level of risk it finds acceptable for a given credit product. There is no single "cutoff score" used by all lenders, and there are many additional factors that lenders use to determine your actual interest rates.

Your FICO score is calculated from the most recent information on your credit report. Certain sections of your credit report provide the information needed to come up with your score. Things such as your identifying information do not count toward your score, nor do soft pulls. A "soft pull" is when you pull your own report or a current lender pulls your report for review.

One section on your credit report that does matter is your public information section. This section provides information on any judgments, liens, or bankruptcies. The next section that really matters is the section that has your account history. Lastly, there is the section that lists your hard pulls. A "hard pull" is when you are looking for credit and someone runs your report. That matters too.

Improving your credit score

Typically having a low credit score means that you are considered a high risk to lenders. Therefore, to compensate for the higher risk, you are usually charged a higher premium. In addition to a higher premium, you could also get charged more fees and higher interest rates on loans of all types. When it comes to improving your score, the first thing that you have to remember is that your score changes as often as your report does. Because most creditors report information to the credit reporting agencies monthly, it is safe to say that your score could change as often as monthly. To improve your score, the first thing you must do is to be patient with the process and let time work to your benefit. This process could feel like watching paint dry, but if you are consistent with following healthy credit habits, your score will change—and probably faster than you think. Then you will be on your way to good credit. Before getting into the specifics of improving your credit score, let me also say that having good credit is a direct byproduct of all the things that were discussed earlier in this book. To explain what a byproduct is, I had to ask my engineer wife to tell me how the process works, and this is what she told me. A by-product by definition is a secondary or incidental product that comes from the manufacturing process of another product, and in most cases is not the primary product or service being produced.

A good example of a by-product is sawdust. As a result of cutting or manufacturing wood for some other use, sawdust is created. No one would destroy a piece of wood just to create sawdust. It just happens as the result of some other process. It is also helpful that sawdust can serve several other purposes, such as being used as for mulch, kitty litter, and particleboard. All of that is to say that having good credit is the result of getting your financial life in order. If you get organized and live on a budget, you will start to save and not have to use credit cards as a back-up plan. Then you will start to make even better financial decisions, which will allow you to discover that you do have extra money in your budget. It is with those extra funds that you will begin to reduce your debt and live better financially, and because you are living better financially, your credit score will ultimately improve with no extra effort on your part. I think you get the point, so let's move forward. The following are the things that you want to start doing to improve your credit permanently. Again, most of these things you should already be doing as a result of your new-found knowledge.

Fix all errors on your credit report immediately.

One survey reported that some 52 percent of individuals surveyed reported at least one major error on their credit report. You definitely want to fix any area on your credit report that has errors. Remember, you can and should get a free copy of your report by visiting www.annualcreditreport.com. The law now allows you to have a free copy of your credit report once a year, so get your report, check it for errors, and dispute those errors.

Pay your bills on time.

The largest percentage of your credit score (35%) is based on your payment history. You want to build a strong payment history to get your score higher. The longer you go without any late payments, the higher your score will be. This is the best and fastest way to rebuild your credit. Having one thirty-day late payment could decrease your score as much as twenty points. Even if you have had credit problems in the past, depending on the size of the debt and how many creditors you have, a good twelve months of continuous payments on time could get you back on track very quickly.

Back away from the edge.

Reducing your credit card balances will have a noticeable impact on your credit score. The next largest percent of your score (30%) is based on the amount owed to creditors. You never want to max out your credit limit; in fact you want to stay below 50% of your credit limit. So if you have a card with a $3,000 limit, you want the balance to be below the $1,500 mark. Spreading your debt between all of your cards so that you are below 50% of the limit will help improve your score. Also, pay off your debts rather than moving them around. Playing the credit card shell game does not improve your score. This should be reason enough for you to want to start right now and develop a strategy to get out of debt. Be careful when you are closing accounts as well, as you will see in the next section that this could do more harm than good.

Commit, Commit, and Commit.

It is natural to want to close old accounts, but keep in mind that 15 percent of your score is determined by the length of time you've held credit relationships. Opening new cards and closing old ones could affect your credit negatively in the long run. So maintaining a long-term healthy relationship with your creditors will serve you better in the long run. Basically, now that you have credit, you want to keep a couple of cards to continue your history, and only use them occasionally, or not at all.

Look before you leap.

The last thing that you can do to improve your credit score is when you are in the market to make a major purchase, you want to check your credit at least six months in advance before applying for credit. Even though new credit only makes up a small percentage of your score (10%), you still want to manage this portion of your credit score. Every time you apply for credit, your score will be impacted. However, there are some things that you can do to minimize the effect of shopping for credit. Though every hit will count against you, the FICO scoring model tends to ignore mortgages and auto loans that are generated within a thirty-day period, and inquiries made within a fourteen-day period will count as one inquiry.

In the end, credit is a must-have in today's fast-moving economy. In times of crisis, your credit could be one of your most powerful tools. Not only does everyday life hinge on you having good credit, but your future success depends on you having good credit as well. Because you have already created a history of having credit, you must do everything you can to maintain a good credit history. By taking control of your finances, you are already on the road to having better credit.

"Good is not good enough
when better is expected."

— Thomas Fuller

Investment Basics

I have to admit that I was a little reluctant to put this particular chapter in this book. After all, I mainly wanted to inspire you with this book to take a look at your financial situation and do better with your money. I also wanted to address how you view your money. In my opinion, investing money is probably the last thing you want to do while you are getting your finances together. Until you have gotten your debt paid off and you have a substantial emergency fund, you should only look forward to investing your money later. I had all but finished this book when at the last minute; I decided to put in a little information regarding investments. This chapter is written to give you some basic information on the various investment options that are available. Before you decide to invest, I want you to give serious consideration to seeking help from a professional advisor.

When you do sit down with someone to help you with your investments, please make sure the person is willing to teach you about investments, and will not just try to push investments that you don't understand. The main thing that you want to do is to go with your gut—that little part of you that lets you know when something is not right. Different types of savings vehicles allow you to access your money and earn interest. Establishing an emergency fund is the first step in a financial plan. There are several ways you can save money and earn more money with the money you save—and still have access to it, should you need it. First, I want to take a look at the differences between a savings account, a money market account, and a money market fund.

Money Market Funds

Banks, brokerages, and mutual fund companies offer money market mutual funds (MMF). They're most commonly used by people with brokerage accounts who sell a stock and then put the proceeds in a MMF until they decide where to reinvest the cash. But these funds can be used to build cash for an emergency fund or other short-term goals. Money market funds are FDIC insured if you open an account at a bank, and they pay a better rate than a basic bank money market account. Money market mutual funds MMFs are highly regulated and invest in very safe, short-term debt securities, such as certificates of deposits and US treasury bills.

Certificates of Deposit

Once you've grown your liquid savings account to create your emergency fund, you should consider a longer-term investment with a higher yield. CDs pay higher yields than liquid savings accounts, but to earn that extra interest, you need to let the bank hold your money for a specific period of time. As your savings grow and your all-important emergency fund has been established, you can then afford to let the bank lock up some of your savings for a period of time to get a higher return.

The drawback to a CD is that CDs are not liquid; remember that when you purchase a CD, you are tying up your funds for a period of time, and if you cash out early, in most cases you'll lose interest and possibly principal. CDs are most often issued by banks, but can be purchased through banks or a brokerage firm. Some banks might require you to come into the bank to open a CD account; others may let you open one online. Typically, you invest a fixed amount of money for a predetermined length of time called the term, and you are guaranteed your principal plus a fixed amount of interest, which you receive periodically throughout the term. When the term expires, you can cash out the principal and interest, or roll over the CD for another term. You can opt to withdraw the interest payments as they are received. CDs can be purchased for terms of almost any duration, although the most popular are between three months and five years. Almost always, the longer you allow the bank to use your money, the higher your interest rate. Generally, it's not a good idea to buy a CD with a term of more than five years. The interest rate situation could change dramatically during that time and you could get stuck with a long-term, low-rate CD. CDs are deposit accounts and are insured by the FDIC up to $250,000.

Investing in Bonds

Bonds are another building block of your investment portfolio. There are several types of bond instruments to choose from and different ways to buy them. Everybody and every entity can buy bonds. Bonds are used by your municipality to fund a new school or by corporations that need to raise money. When you buy a bond, you're lending your money. A bond, according to Webster's dictionary, is an interest-bearing certificate issued by a government or business promising to pay the holder a specified sum on a specified date. US treasury bills, notes, and bonds are excellent, risk-free ways to preserve your principal, get pretty good returns, and keep your investments relatively liquid.

The US government sells treasury securities called bills, notes, and savings bonds. These bonds are available on the open market, and all of these bonds are debt instruments sold to raise money to operate the government and pay off debt. Treasury securities are safe investments, because they're backed by the US government. The minimum amount required to buy a treasury bill or note is

$1,000. Savings bonds can be purchased for as little as $25. Treasury bills (T-bills) are short-term securities that mature in one year or less, and you buy them for less than par (face) value. When the bill matures, you receive par value. For example, you might buy a $10,000 26-week T-bill for $9,750. If you hold it until maturity, you'll be paid $10,000. That extra $250 is the interest you earned. Treasury notes usually mature in two to ten years.

Corporate Bonds

Sometimes companies need to borrow money, and one of the ways they raise the funds is by selling bonds. When you buy a corporate bond, you are loaning money to a company.

Corporate bonds are risky when compared to other fixed-income securities, because they are backed by the corporation itself, and in some cases, companies are more likely than governments to have serious financial problems. Corporations reward you for taking the extra risk by paying a higher interest rate than you would get on most government securities.

The interest rate you receive is called the coupon. If you hold the bond until maturity, you'll receive the face value of the bond—assuming the company doesn't default. If you sell the bond before maturity, you risk losing principal if interest rates have risen. Bond prices fall when interest rates rise, and conversely, bond prices rise when interest rates fall. If you buy a ten-year bond with a face value of $5,000 and a coupon, or interest rate, of 6 percent, and then decide to sell it after three years when interest rates have risen to 8 percent, no one would want to pay you the full value of your bond, because new bonds would be paying higher interest. Of course, if rates have fallen by the time you decide to cash your bond, you could get a premium for it, because your bond would be paying more interest than new bonds. When it comes to corporate bonds, the main drawback is that there is not a guaranteed return of principal as there is with government bonds that are held to maturity.

Stocks: Sharing a Corporation

Stocks are pieces of the corporate pie. When you buy shares of stocks, you own a slice of the company, which is considered an equity investment. If you buy stock in a corporation, you typically have an ownership share in that corporation and are described as a stockholder or shareholder. You buy stock because you expect it to increase in value, or because you expect the corporation to pay you dividend income, or a portion of its profits. In fact, many stocks provide the potential for both growth and income. When a corporation issues stock, it gets the proceeds from that initial sale. After that, shares of the stock are traded, or bought and sold among investors, but the corporation gets no additional income. The price of the stock moves up or down, depending on how much you and other investors are willing to pay for it at the time.

Common Stock

Most of the stocks sold in the US are common stock. Owning common stock entitles you to dividends from the corporation. Owning a stock also allows you to sell your stock at a profit if its price increases, and to vote for the board of directors. Common stock prices aren't fixed, so they can lose value as well as gain. Despite the risk associated with owning stocks, investors are willing to buy common stock because over time stocks in general—though not every individual stock—have provided a stronger return than have other investments. *Blue chip* is a term borrowed from poker, where the blue chips are the most valuable. Blue chip stocks are those of the largest, most consistently profitable corporations. The list isn't official, and it does change.

Mutual Funds

One of the best and least risky ways to purchase and own a stock is to purchase shares of a mutual fund. A mutual fund is a pool of money funded by several investors who want to own equity investments, such as stock. The way the process works is that a group of investors initially choose to pool their money together with the intent of investing in stocks.

The funds are then turned over to a team of experts and analysts, headed by a fund manager. The manager, with the help of his or her team, searches for the best stocks to purchase based on the criteria set forth in the fund. In other words, some funds choose to only invest in larger, more established companies that have a long history of earnings, and they are the least risky of equity investments. These companies are called large capitalization companies. Therefore, that type of fund is called a Large Cap fund, and the money is only invested in that type of stock. What makes these investments so appealing to many individuals is that mutual funds provide an easy way to enter the market without a great deal of additional work on their part. There are other benefits to investing in mutual funds as well. By pooling money from a number of people, a mutual fund can provide greater buying power for each investor. And, because the fund buys and sells several hundred securities at a time, its brokerage costs are often lower than you would pay as an individual investor. Other benefits of investing in mutual funds include, but are not limited to the following. When you invest in mutual funds, your investment is subject to the all of the risk associated with buying stock, but just on a smaller scale. Once a mutual fund has been established, its shares are bought and sold on the market just as are individual stocks. The greatest benefit of investing in mutual funds is diversification.

Diversification

A mutual fund invests in several hundred securities at one time. It would be difficult for the average investor to buy such a wide variety of investments individually, because the cost would be prohibitive. Owning several different securities—including stocks, bonds, and cash equivalents (money market instruments)—helps in managing your overall risk.

Professional Money Management

When you buy shares in a mutual fund, you automatically get full-time professional money management. The fund's manager, with the help of a dedicated team of analysts, analyze hundreds of securities and makes decisions on what to buy, when to buy, and when to sell. With professional management, once you've chosen a fund that's right for you, there's no need to constantly monitor the stock market or economic conditions in order to make changes—the portfolio manager does it for you.

Affordability and Liquidity

You can usually invest in a mutual fund for a low minimum initial investment—sometimes as low as $250—and make subsequent investments in small increments—sometimes as little as $50 per month. You can sell shares of an open-end mutual fund on almost any business day. You don't have to wait for the fund company to find a buyer for your shares, because it is ready to issue new shares or redeem existing shares at any time. Keep in mind that the price of all mutual fund shares can change daily, and you'll receive the current value of your shares when you sell—and that price may be more or less than your original cost.

Common Goals

Another great benefit of mutual funds is that you don't have to feel as if you are in this thing alone. Whether your goal is a regular source of income, your child's education, or a comfortable retirement, there's a fund designed to meet your needs. Matching your goals with the goals outlined in the fund's prospectus is an important step, and you can get help from your financial advisor. Stock funds should only be considered for the long-term; bond funds should be considered when a stream of income is desired. Some funds, including non-diversified funds and funds investing in international securities, high yield bonds, small- and mid-cap stocks and/or more volatile segments of the economy, entail additional risk and may not be appropriate for all investors. Consult a fund's prospectus for additional information on these and other risks.

Dollar Cost Averaging

An Automatic Investment Plan (AIP) lets you automatically transfer a preset amount of money from your bank account into a fund that you choose at regular intervals. Because mutual funds are so affordable, many investors choose to invest in mutual funds regularly by using an AIP. You determine how much you want to invest and how often. Because it's automatic, an AIP ensures that you reach your long-term goals before you're tempted to spend those assets on a new suit or a set of golf clubs.

An AIP gives investing for your future the same importance as your other periodic payments—your monthly bills, for example. As a result, you're much more likely to stick with your plan until you reach your goal because you invest the same amount in a fund at regular intervals over time. You could potentially buy more shares when the price is lower and fewer shares when the price is higher by letting your AIP run.

By setting up an AIP, you will reduce your average cost per share over time. This strategy, called "dollar cost averaging," helps make market fluctuations work for you, and reduces the risk that you'll invest all your money right before a market downturn. Dollar cost averaging offers its greatest benefit with investments that tend to regularly fluctuate in price, which is why Automatic Investment Plans can be especially effective when used in conjunction with stock funds. The share price of these funds can vary widely, but through dollar cost averaging, an AIP can help make this volatility work for you.

As you can see, I am a huge fan of mutual fund investing. By investing in mutual funds, you gain access to the stock market's growth potential, and you may reduce your cost of investing over the long term.

"All that you accomplish or fail to accomplish with your life is the direct result of your thoughts."

— James Allen

Final Thoughts

Op-por-tu-ni-ty — *a situation or condition favorable for attainment of a goal.* I once heard a speaker say, "Missed opportunities are the curse of potential." Judging by the definition of the word opportunity, I have to agree with that speaker. By now, I hope that the words in this book have motivated you to change not only your financial situation, but also your thoughts on how you handle your money. Now you have been presented with an opportunity to do something different. Will you take advantage of that opportunity, or will you pass on this opportunity as you have with so many other chances that have already come and gone?

Most of us are surrounded by opportunities to become successful, but many of those opportunities go unrealized. In his book, *Acres of Diamonds*, author Russell Conwell tells the story of Ali Hefed, a Persian farmer who had wealth beyond his wildest imagination, yet with all of his wealth, Ali was still not content. One day, after speaking with a Buddhist priest and learning of a land that was littered with acres of diamonds, Ali got excited about the idea of having even more wealth, so he sold his fertile farm and traveled the world in search of the "acres of diamonds." Ali spent a lifetime searching for the acres of diamonds, and he eventually died in poverty and despair in a distant land. In the meantime, the famed beds of Golconda diamonds were found on his abandoned farm.

My Story

Earlier I alluded to the story of how my wife and I almost went broke before we woke up financially. My story actually starts way before the moment my wife and I started making financial mistakes. I was born in Birmingham, Alabama, and growing up it was basically my mother and me. I watched my mother make bad financial decisions, and when I became an adult, I continued to make bad financial decisions. I remember being in the United States Marine Corps and getting to my first permanent duty station in Camp Pendleton, California. After being mostly confined to the base for the first couple months of my assignment, I desperately wanted a car, and would have done anything to get one. It was then that my lack of financial literacy showed itself, I wanted a car so badly that I borrowed $550 dollars from the local credit union, and put that with the other money that I had saved, then used it all as a down payment to purchase my first car. What's wrong with doing something like that, you may ask? Well basically I borrowed money to go out and borrow even more money. Not only did I have a car payment and an insurance payment, I also had a loan payment. By the time I was done, I had paid way more than the car was worth. I had to pay back the car loan plus interest, as well as the personal loan plus interest, which made this a really bad idea in the long run.

That was not my finest hour, and sadly, many more bad financial decisions were made before I finally woke up to the reality that if I didn't do something different, my life was going to continue to spiral downward, financially. Despite making over $100,000 per year between the two of us, at one point, my wife and I were two months behind on our mortgage payment. The reason we found ourselves in that position was because we had never been formally educated about personal finance. I have a B.S. degree in finance, and I was a financial advisor, so naturally I thought I had it all together. In other words, my wife and I were normal. You see, in this country, normal is having a mortgage that you can't afford and two car payments that you shouldn't have. Then, when you don't have the money to buy the things you want, you just finance it. That's the American way.

We typically buy the things we desire on credit—not the things we need. When we pay our rent or mortgage, we typically use cash. When we make a car payment, we tend to use cash. Even when we go to the grocery store, we usually pay in cash. These are all things that we legitimately need in order to have a decent life. But when it comes to buying that flat screen TV that we simply want, we somehow justify financing it. In fact, in most cases, when we walk into our favorite electronics store, we see the monthly payment posted right in front of the TV. To build wealth, we have to stop saying, "How much per month?" We need to start asking, simply, "How much?" It's not really a good deal if we have to turn around and finance the item; it only feels like a deal at that moment.

Think for a moment how different would your life be if you didn't have all the payments that you are currently making. Imagine getting your paycheck and only having to pay the normal living expenses, such as water, electricity, food, and shelter. What would you do with the extra money? How would your life change? The next question is, "What's stopping you from paying off those current bills that you have accumulated? The answer—you!

Do Something!

Today is the day that you decided to do something different. No longer will you continue to lie on the nail and whimper every time you move, because it hurts a little. It needs to hurt more than a little. It needs to hurt a lot, and it needs to hurt enough for you to want to do something about it.

There are three frogs on a log and one of the frogs decides to jump off. How many frogs remain on the log?

If you answered *two*, then you are *wrong!* The answer is *three*. Deciding to do something and actually doing it are two different things. Every day people decide that they are going to do something, but then never do it. To be successful in this thing we call life, we have to not only decide to do something, we have to develop a plan of action and get about the business of making it happen. The way I see it, people are generally divided into three categories: those who watch things happen, those who wonder what happened, and those who make things happen.

Do something today to change your tomorrow. If you don't, then your tomorrow will be the same as your yesterday. — Lonnie Mathews

Successful people make things happen by taking action and not allowing themselves to get distracted by things and obstacles that get in the way. It's about developing a passion about doing better with your finances, and then turning that passion it to commitment. The biggest difference between those who are successful and those who aren't is that successful people are passionate about their commitments. Successful people are not complacent with where they are, and they don't procrastinate in doing the things that are required of them to be successful. Most of all, successful people are willing to make the necessary sacrifices to be successful and are will to pay the cost.

When it comes to achieving success, you have to be willing to pay the cost associated with success. If building wealth is your desire right now, I want you decide how much money you would like to have and in what time you period you would like to have it. Write that information on a sheet of paper, and put it where you can see it every day. When you have done these things, you are on your way to building wealth. There is one final thing that I want you to do, and that is: *Determine what you intend to give up in return for building the wealth you desire.* There is no such thing as "something for nothing."

Resources

Every effort is being taken to recognize any references made to other authors included in this book. While the views and opinions expressed in this book are original works of mine, some of the views and opinions that I have developed over the years were in some way impacted by the works in the references section

In addition to the resources used to create this book, I would also like to take this opportunity to recommend the following must read" books to help you form a healthy mindset for handling your finances.

Dave Ramsey – *Financial Peace*

Ron Blue & Jeremy White – *Surviving Financial Meltdown*

Robert Kiyosaki – *Rich Dad Poor Dad*

References

Conwell, R. Acres of Diamonds.
Clauson, G. S. The Richest Man in Babylon.
Mandino, O. The Greatest Salesman in The World.
McCormack, M. What They Don't Teach You in Harvard Business School
Parkinson, C. N. Parkinson's Law.
Stewart Welch / Larry Waschka. Getting Rich.
Stanley, Thomas D. W. The Millionaire Next Door.

About the Author

As a child growing up in a single-parent home in Birmingham, Alabama, Lonnie R. Mathews dreamed of having an impact on people's lives. Shortly after high school, Lonnie joined the United States Marine Corps, where he successfully served eight years. He is a veteran of Desert Shield and Desert Storm. Lonnie was honorably discharged on December 2, 1992, and enrolled at the University of Alabama Tuscaloosa, where he graduated with a bachelor of science degree in finance and a master's degree in accounting from Strayer University.

Lonnie developed a passion for personal finance after learning and understanding the exciting and mysterious world of finance. With persistence and determination, Lonnie continues a process of self-education that has distinguished him as an authority on personal finance and the process of getting out of debt. To realize his passion, Lonnie has held positions as a financial analyst and as a financial planner.

Entertaining and Motivating Speaker

Lonnie Mathews is fast becoming recognized as an exciting and inspirational speaker. Being in debt most of his adult life, Lonnie and his wife quickly realized that this was not God's plan for their finances. After much prayer and seeking God in their finances, Lonnie and his wife took the necessary steps to become debt free. As a result of his newfound freedom, Lonnie published his first of many books on personal financial freedom and financial peace, titled Beating Debt & Building Wealth, a financial guide for Christians. As a premier keynote speaker, Lonnie now travels the country delivering his powerful and life changing messages.

Successful Author and Entrepreneur

In 2000, Lonnie co-founded Alliance Financial Ministries, a non-profit financial literacy company. The goal of this company is to provide individuals with the education and tools necessary to make sound financial decisions. Alliance Financial provides seminars, motivational tapes, motivational materials, and workshops nationally.